ESTATE PLANNING
FOR PEOPLE WITH A
CHRONIC CONDITION
OR DISABILITY

ESTATE PLANNING
FOR PEOPLE WITH A
CHRONIC CONDITION
OR DISABILITY

MARTIN M. SHENKMAN, CPA, MBA, JD

demosHEALTH

Visit our web site at www.demosmedpub.com

Medical information provided by Demos Health, in the absence of a visit with a healthcare professional, must be considered as an educational service only. This book is not designed to replace a physician's independent judgment about the appropriateness or risks of a procedure or therapy for a given patient. Our purpose is to provide you with information that will help you make your own healthcare decisions.

The information and opinions provided here are believed to be accurate and sound, based on the best judgment available to the authors, editors, and publisher, but readers who fail to consult appropriate health authorities assume the risk of any injuries. The publisher is not responsible for errors or omissions. The editors and publisher welcome any reader to report to the publisher any discrepancies or inaccuracies noticed.

Library of Congress Cataloging-in-Publication Data
Shenkman, Martin M.
  Estate planning : for people with a chronic condition or disability / Martin M. Shenkman.
       p. cm.
  Includes index.
  ISBN-13: 978-1-932603-66-8 (pbk. : alk. paper)
  ISBN-10: 1-932603-66-2 (pbk. : alk. paper)
  1. Estate planning--United States. 2. People with disabilities--Legal status, laws, etc.--United States. 3. Trusts and trustees--United States. I. Title.
  KF750.S475 2009
  346.7305'2--dc22

                    2008046922

Special discounts on bulk quantities of Demos Medical Publishing books are available to corporations, professional associations, pharmaceutical companies, health care organizations, and other qualifying groups. For details, please contact:

   Special Sales Department
   Demos Medical Publishing
   386 Park Avenue South, Suite 301
   New York, NY 10016
   Phone: 800–532–8663 or 212–683–0072
   Fax: 212–683–0118
   E-mail: orderdept@demosmedpub.com

Made in the United States of America
09 10 11 12   5 4 3 2

DEDICATION

Martin Luther King, Jr., in his book, *Where Do We Go from Here? Chaos or Community,* made the following observation: "We have inherited a large house . . . a great 'worldhouse' in which we have to live together—black and white, Easterner and Westerner, Gentile and Jew, Catholic and Protestant, Muslim and Hindu . . . a family separated by ideas, culture, and interest who . . . must learn somehow to live with each other in peace."

The idea of "diversity" has slowly come to the fore. To the extent that we can embrace the uniqueness of each of us in a positive manner, each of us and the world as a whole will benefit in tremendous ways. But diversity must encompass more than gender, race, religion, and culture. True diversity must encompass all the characteristics that make each of us so unique and special, including the special attributes of disability. Often, those who struggle with a health issue have the insight to savor the moment, to appreciate the simple and beautiful things in life that so many others take for granted. My wonderful wife Patti is an awe-inspiring embodiment of these attributes. Too often, however, those who are fortunate enough to be healthy lack the compassion and empathy that should be the core of what being human is about.

Thus, this book is dedicated to all of those who help bring the message of diversity to the world—diversity that encompasses the array of tragic, and sometimes hopeful, health issues so many struggle with. In particular, this book is dedicated to those bringing this message of essential humanity to those so needing to hear it.

❖ Perhaps one day, when one receives a devastating diagnosis, that pain will be comforted, not compounded, by friends, family, supposed loved ones, employers, and society as a whole.

❖ Perhaps one day, each family member of someone struck with a severe illness will run to support, not run to hide.

❖ Perhaps one day, the pushy people in line at an amusement park and supermarket will pause long enough before pushing to contemplate that someone in line with them may have a balance problem or other health issue to cope with.

❖ Perhaps one day, all employers will do more than just show the compassion that their training, positions, education, and stations warrant; they will actively seek out those with disabilities for the special humanity they bring to the workplace.

❖ Perhaps one day, lawyers advocating for employers of those with disabilities and health issues will take pause long enough to consider the human suffering on the other end of the equation before charging full-speed ahead to zealously serve their clients, rather than the persons in true need. Perhaps one day, zealous representation will be used as originally intended, rather than as a shield to protect what is often little more than financial pursuits.

Above all, this book is dedicated to all those living with chronic illness who inspire us all to support them in their noble cause. All royalties will be donated to this cause.

CONTENTS

Introduction

WHAT IS ESTATE PLANNING?

Estate planning is all about giving you peace of mind about a host of problems that may confront you during your lifetime and affect your loved ones thereafter. Estate planning means planning to protect you from legal, financial, and other problems. It's about a lot more than signing a will. A simple e-mail from a woman living with multiple sclerosis provides a great example of the depth, detail, personal issues, and more that must be addressed to develop an estate plan.

WHAT QUESTIONS DO YOU HAVE?

The following e-mail, received from a woman named Bonnie in response to an article on financial powers of attorney for those living with chronic illness, embodies many of the issues, misinformation, personal struggles, and practical issues faced by someone living with a chronic illness. Let Bonnie's questions introduce this book and the need for special steps to help so many like her. Whether the issues you face, the questions you have, or the documents you need are the same as Bonnie's, the reality of her situation and questions will hit home. Her inquisitive and thought-provoking e-mail, received as the finishing touches were being made to this book, seemed to be the ideal introduction. Providing practical solutions to help the Bonnies in this country is the goal of this book.

BONNIE'S E-MAIL

Dear Mr. Shenkman,

My name is Bonnie, I am 49 and live in _____ (state name). I am also the unfortunate recipient of multiple sclerosis (MS) and have had it now for almost 20 years. Although I am mobile, my health has somewhat declined, which is quite scary.

The reason I am writing you today is because I am quite concerned about a few different things and thought maybe you could point me in the right direction.

I am a homeowner and am concerned about who will get my home when I pass. I made a will from a will kit my friend sent me through the mail, being particularly careful to follow instructions. I am unable to obtain a lawyer at the moment since after working 32 years, I am no longer able to work per doctor's orders. This is kind of scary for me since I have always been very self-sufficient working 2 jobs, sometimes 3 at a time. I finally was able to purchase my home 14 years ago when I was still quite mobile and working full time. One never knows when it comes to your health what can happen.

I left instructions that my home go to my mother since she is still alive and thankfully healthy. She is my only living relative, although I do have one brother, from whom I am estranged. If she predeceases me, then it is left to one friend of mine who currently resides in New York.

On the other hand, my mom was told by a lawyer that because of my disability, I must have whatever monies/property is left to me put into a trust. Then the monies can be allocated to me whenever necessary, providing I state what the need is.

I am baffled by this since my physical condition cannot be predicted, but my mental state is sharp and clear. Why should money have to be allocated to me? And what if nothing was ever said to a lawyer about my disability?

The problem my mother is having is finding someone for a trust for me and this is weighing heavily on her.

I know you must be extremely busy and rightfully so, but I would greatly appreciate a reply from you regarding these matters. It would be of great comfort to both myself as well as my mother.

Many thanks for reading this, and I anxiously await your reply,

Bonnie

REPLY TO BONNIE

Bonnie faces many of the same issues and struggles of many living with a chronic illness.

❖ *My name is Bonnie, I am 49 and live in* _____. Bonnie needs to consult an attorney specializing in estate planning in the state in which she resides. State laws, and the programs various states afford to those with health issues, differ substantially. Be wary of relying on any web site or on a standardized form. Even the sample forms and discussions in this book, although designed and intended to help you get a plan and documents in place, must always be reviewed by an attorney in your state. The generic Internet documents, while cheap (perhaps their only attribute), are not tailored to address the local nuances that a local expert will understand.

❖ *I am also the unfortunate recipient of multiple sclerosis (MS) and have had it now for almost 20 years. Although I am mobile, my health has somewhat declined, which is quite scary.* Declining health is scary for anyone. It means losing control over matters you could formerly deal with. However, putting your financial and legal house in order, getting in place a comprehensive financial plan and the right estate planning documents to protect you, and simplifying your assets so that they are easier to manage as your health continues to decline will give you assurance and some certainty in what is otherwise an uncertain life.

❖ *The reason I am writing you today is because I am quite concerned about a few different things and thought maybe you could point me in the right direction.* The right direction will be different for each person's unique circumstances. But there are some common threads that form the backbone of this book and should be in everyone's plan:

Documents. You need to have the same documents that everyone else has, modified to address chronic illness and tailored to your circumstances. There is a chapter on each of the key documents.

Financial plan. You need a comprehensive financial plan that addresses your financial needs, the impact of your illness, the likely course your illness will take, and other possible scenarios and contingencies for which to plan. This book addresses financial planning only tangentially, as it affects your estate planning. But contrary to how most estate planners operate, estate plans and financial plans are inextricably linked. You really cannot plan your estate if you don't have a financial plan. Conversely, your financial plan, especially if you have a chronic illness, is unlikely to be successful if you don't have a proper estate plan.

❖   *I am a homeowner and am concerned about who will get my home when I pass.* A home is often the largest asset many people have. What your will or other estate planning document provides for must be coordinated with the ownership of your property (called "title" in legal jargon). What is on your deed? Too often people spend time and money on a will to transfer their home on death when either the deed bypasses their estate or could have accomplished the same result more efficiently. If the deed for your house lists "Bonnie and Mom, as joint tenants with right of survivorship," then on your death, Mom would get the house. No probate, no will, no hassle. However, relying on that alone can be dangerous. What if mom predeceases? Who gets the house then? If your disability advances to the point where you cannot make decisions, it would be better for the house to be held in a revocable living trust to facilitate the management of the property for your benefit. On the other hand, if your target beneficiary is younger than you and really likely to survive you, a simple deed might just be the ticket.

❖   *I made a will from a will kit my friend sent me through the mail, being particularly careful to follow instructions.* Whoa there, partner. Hold your horses! This is one of those "do not pass go, do not collect $200" cards. You're really picking from the "Chance" pile on that one. Internet and will kit forms are cheap, but they are no substitute for competent professional advice. Did the will kit ask you what your deed said? If your deed lists your ex-husband, recent boyfriend, or your mother as a joint owner, your will may not have any impact on what happens to your house. Did your will kit talk about insurance? Did it address whether you have the financial wherewithal to hold onto your house? What about managing your house if you were to become fully incapacitated? That's what a plan prepared by professionals does and a will kit does not do. What does your power of attorney say about selling your house? Who is your agent who can make those decisions? Will kits don't address that. Significantly, no fill-in-the-blank form or computer program can yet substitute for the knowledge and wisdom of decades of experience, nor address the nuances of your health situation. Some of the material prepared

KEY

Far more important for you, Bonnie, is that there are a collection of other issues pertaining to your house to address as part of your plan. Remember, estate planning done right is not just about a will or bequeathing property. Do you have adequate property and liability coverage? Do you have an umbrella or personal excess liability policy? This is usually pretty inexpensive and can be vital to protect your assets if there is ever a lawsuit.

For example, if a car accident is triggered by an impairment or attack attributable to an illness, the costs associated with a lawsuit could exceed the coverage available under the impaired driver's automobile insurance policy and jeopardize other assets, including the driver's home! An umbrella liability policy can protect against that and might be vital for individuals with a chronic illness who push the envelope by driving beyond the time they really should be doing so. Many people living with chronic illness continue to drive until an "event" convinces them to stop or a loved one makes them stop. Getting an umbrella policy could be one of the most important steps they can take to safeguard their future.

Finally, remember the old saying, "A man's home is his castle." For someone with a chronic illness, that castle could really be an irreplaceable bastion of comfort and security. If you've modified your home to include an office where you can work, all the accommodations that you might need, room for a caretaker, and so on, steps to preserve and safeguard your home may be far more important for you than for the average castle-owner. So, while it is important to consider what happens when you die, you're only 49, multiple sclerosis may not have a significant impact on your life expectancy, and there are much bigger fish to fry than worrying about a will. Unfortunately, most estate planners focus on wills and transferring assets. Remember the words in the Paul Simon song: "Get a plan, Stan." That will serve you much better then the old adage, "Where there's a will, there's a way."

using canned forms and web sites is so bad that it is literally worse than not having a document. Will kits and web sites can, however, be used in one really productive way—as tools to make many or most of the decisions you need to make before a lawyer turns his clock on. The more prepared you are the better the end product you'll get and at less cost. But canned forms can never identify and address the planning nuances unique to you.

❖ *I am unable to obtain a lawyer at the moment since after working 32 years, I am no longer able to work per doctor's orders.* Bonnie, you probably can't afford *not* to get the right advice. The results could be devastating. There are some great resources available, and hopefully this book will serve as the catalyst for many organizations to run an "estate planning day" with local professionals volunteering time to help the tens of millions of people just like you. Hopefully, many of the questions raised in this chapter will help you and others understand the vital importance of getting the right help and give you an understanding of what that might entail.

❖ *This is kind of scary for me since I have always been very self-sufficient working 2 jobs, sometimes 3 at a time.* It is disconcerting. But getting a real plan together will help keep you in control and ensure your future. Whatever the future holds, however difficult, it will always be better if planned. You sound like a real fighter, and that's great. That's the spirit that will keep you going. Your comment points out a really significant misconception most financial planners, estate planners, accountants, and other advisers have about those with chronic illness. Most immediately assume that the chronically ill have few assets or work history. Most estate planners assume family members need to set up a special needs trust for the chronically ill loved one. Most financial planners assume that a client with chronic illness has no resources and needs short-term conservative investments, even if the opposite might be true (as it is for you, Bonnie). Many advisers assume that those with chronic illness have no expertise or business knowledge. You clearly have expertise and knowledge from years of work and, hopefully, some significant assets (your home is one) that warrant the respect and planning they deserve. Those with a chronic illness unfortunately have to insist on getting the respect and proper guidance they need and make sure that advice is tailored to their circumstances, and not tailored in a way that reflects some adviser's generic misconceptions about clients with chronic illness.

❖   *I finally was able to purchase my home 14 years ago when I was still quite mobile and working full time.* After 14 years, your home has likely appreciated substantially in value and you've hopefully paid down much of your mortgage. While you might be too young for a reverse mortgage to augment your cash flow, talking with a skilled financial planner might give you some important ideas. Depending on your other assets and resources, you might be just fine if you budget carefully. If the numbers don't work, the sooner you analyze the "what if" scenarios the better. For example, selling your house, downsizing to cut costs, and investing the difference might make your financial picture workable. There are myriad scenarios. These are all more important than the issue of who inherits your house.

❖   *One never knows when it comes to your health what can happen.* You said it. No one. That is why everyone should plan yesterday, before the problems of tomorrow get here.

❖   *I left instructions that my home go to my mother since she is still alive and thankfully healthy. She is my only living relative, although I do have one brother, from whom I am estranged. If she predeceases me, then it is left to one friend of mine who currently resides in New York.* See the comments above concerning the deed, a revocable trust, and so on. Informal instructions can have no impact on who would receive your house on death. Instructions in a will might determine where your house will go, but only if the deed results in your will governing the disposition of your house. But neither informal instructions nor a will (even if the deed leaves the will in control) address how your house is to be managed if you become too disabled to manage it yourself or deal with the financial planning and insurance issues, and so on. The situation with your brother is sad, especially in light of your health struggles. Whatever family slights or perceived slights occurred in the past, it is too bad that he cannot put them behind him and be there to help you out. Many suffering with chronic illnesses find that family members, close friends, and even a partner or a spouse disappear when the going gets tough. This is why a comprehensive estate and financial plan is so vital. You need to address who will help you if you need it and to have several alternates (called "successor agents" or "successor fiduciaries") if the people you named cannot or will not help. If your funds are adequate, it is ideal to name a professional fiduciary (such as a bank or trust company) in a living trust to manage your assets if and when you cannot do so. Finally, what about leaving your house to a charity that is dedicated to combating and looking for a cure for your disease instead of just a friend? Perhaps you can split the value of the house and your remaining assets between mom, your friend, and a charity. Making a commitment today, even if it is not paid until after your death (this is called a "planned gift" or a "deferred gift") can help boost the fund-raising efforts of the charity you choose.

❖ *On the other hand, my Mom was told by a lawyer that because of my disability, I must have whatever monies/property is left to me put in a trust. Then the monies can be allocated to me whenever necessary providing I state what the need is.* Maybe yes, maybe no. This advice might be based on the prevailing misconception most advisers hold, that folks with chronic illness have few resources. We won't list the myriad accomplished, and often wealthy, folks with chronic illnesses to prove the point. If you are receiving government aid, then in fact if your mother left you assets outright, those assets could disqualify you for the aid and the programming essential for you. In that case, your mother's bequest to you could be made in a special trust, called a "special needs trust" or SNT.

Let's define the lingo. A trust is really a contractual arrangement in which a person called a "trustee" is designated to manage assets of the trust (called "corpus"). These assets are managed for you (the "beneficiary"). A special needs trust restricts the trustee's rights to make distributions to you to only those items and purposes that are above and beyond basic living expenses. Governmental programs would provide these if you had inadequate resources and met their qualifications. If, however, you own a home which might have significant equity and have other assets from your many years of work experience, a special needs trust might be an unnecessary restriction on you. If you had a chronic illness that would assuredly result in significant cognitive impact making it impossible at some point for you to make your own decisions, then a trust would certainly make sense. Finally, you raised the issue about funds being allocated to you. Depending on the nature of the trust being set up for you under your mother's will (or perhaps a trust established for you during her lifetime, independent of her will), you could be a cotrustee along with a bank, trust company, or friend, and you could have the right to make certain distributions to yourself under the trust. So be careful with generic advice. It might work for vitamins, but not for estate plans.

❖ *I am baffled by this since my physical condition cannot be predicted, but my mental state is sharp and clear. Why should money have to be allocated to me? And what if nothing was ever said to a lawyer about my disability?* Trusts, when properly set up, are the ideal way to inherit money, health issue or not! A properly crafted trust can provide any or all of the following benefits:

Protection against lawsuits ("asset protection"). Like the car accident example used earlier, for those with a chronic illness this might be more important than for those without health issues.

Estate taxes. If someone is sufficiently wealthy, inheriting assets in a trust may enable that person to access those assets without being subject to estate tax. Bonnie, while you feel cash strapped, the equity in your home alone, depending on where you live, could subject your estate to a state level estate tax. If this is compounded by money you inherit from your mother, you still might face an estate tax even if you feel you are financially insecure.

Management. Naming a cotrustee (to serve with you) can provide essential help to anyone, but especially to someone living with a chronic illness. For example, if you develop cognitive issues as a result of MS, inheriting assets in a trust with you and a major bank as co-trustees is a great way to involve you in your own finances and decision making for as long as possible. The institutional cotrustee can handle all investments, bill paying, paperwork, and other administrative matters for you when that becomes necessary. You can be issued monthly reports and have full joint decision making. This can be far safer than inheriting assets outright and struggling to manage them alone well past the point when you need help. Too often, those with cognitive or other health issue are taken advantage of, even by family members. If you inherit outright and don't have adequate estate planning documents to protect you, a court might appoint a guardian to manage your person and/or property. You might feel estranged from your brother, but that might not stop him from resurfacing and trying to convince a court that he is your "loving brother" concerned with your well being. If he is the only living family member, if something happens to your mother, then a court may buy into his petition! Setting up a trust for you in your mother's will, ensuring that you have appropriate documents and planning, and including references in your estate planning documents confirming your estranged relationship, can all ensure against this happening. It is not uncommon for an estranged sibling to endeavor to cause harm or win some long-forgotten power play in this manner.

❖   *The problem my mother is having is finding someone for a trust for me and this is weighing heavily on her.* If there are adequate assets, use a bank or a professional trust company, naming that institution and you as co-trustees. That is often the safest and best approach. If your mom has to reach to identify persons that can serve as trustees, they may not be the people you really want to rely upon.

❖   *I know you must be extremely busy and rightfully so, but I would greatly appreciate a reply from you regarding these matters. It would be of great comfort to both myself as well as my mother.* Peace of mind, or comfort, is really the goal of every estate and financial plan. That is why a comprehensive approach is the best way to achieve that comfort. The challenge is to do this in a cost-effective manner that is tailored to reflect the nuances of your illness. Hopefully your extraordinarily comprehensive and insightful questions, which we've analyzed in some detail here, will serve as a guide for many others struggling with similar issues and challenges.

CHAPTER SUMMARY

Dig in like Bonnie. Think through your concerns and questions. Take the risk Bonnie did by opening up and revealing her personal thoughts. Admit what worries you. If you are scared and can say why, that is the first step to getting the help and guidance you need. Remember that the most important question in estate and financial planning is "what if?" Ask lots of questions, make sure you understand the answers, and also make sure that in the end, like Bonnie, you find the steps to lead you to the "comfort zone" you want and deserve. Whatever chronic illness you are living with, the general planning concepts in this book will help guide you.

CHAPTER 1

7 Steps of Estate Planning

Introduction to the 7 Steps

IF YOU OR A LOVED ONE UNDERTAKE ESTATE PLANNING, there are seven key steps to consider in the process. These steps are discussed below, and then followed by a more detailed discussion of how these steps change if you (or your loved one) is living with a chronic illness, as 90 million Americans are. The difference between how these steps are applied for people in general, versus those with a chronic illness, will help highlight the special nature of planning for those living with a chronic disease.

7 Estate Planning Steps to Protect Everyone

KEY

> There are seven key estate planning steps that everyone needs to take to protect themselves from a wide range of estate planning issues and problems. After this general discussion, these concepts will be evaluated from the perspective of how to address them when you have a chronic illness.

○ STEP 1: ORGANIZE EMERGENCY INFORMATION

In an emergency, will your family and loved ones know where key legal, tax and financial information is? Unless you make an effort to organize these records and communicate the information, they won't. Signing a power of attorney to authorize someone to take legal and financial actions for you may not be of much practical help if they cannot figure out where your bank accounts are. Organizing and communicating information is important to your plan succeeding. Take the time to make sure the crucial information that may be needed in an emergency is organized, available, and simple.

○ STEP 2: DESIGNATE A PERSON TO HANDLE FINANCIAL AND LEGAL ISSUES

If you cannot get to the bank to take care of deposits or bills, how will these important issues be tended to? While practical steps such as online bill paying and automatic deposit of checks can help, they are never enough to rely upon. What you need is a legal document, called a power of attorney, in which you can designate a person to handle important legal, tax, and other matters in your place.

○ STEP 3: DESIGNATE A PERSON TO MAKE HEALTH CARE DECISIONS AND ACCESS MEDICAL RECORDS

If you undergo surgery, have an accident, or are rushed into hospital with a medical emergency, who can make medical decisions for you? Once you become an adult, no one has the right to make health care and other decisions for you unless you give them that right. In order to do that, you need a legal document, called a health care proxy. Unless you take the time to prepare an appropriate document, you cannot have any assurance that your health care wishes will be carried out. In some instances you won't need anyone to take over decision making for you, but you may want a trusted friend or family member to monitor your care. For them to have access to your medical records, you will have to provide them with a special authorization to do so. This authorization must address the requirements of the Health Insurance Portability and Accountability Act (HIPAA).

○ STEP 4: COMMUNICATE YOUR HEALTH CARE WISHES

While it is vitally important that you designate someone to make health care decisions for you in case of an emergency, that alone is not enough. What if a decision has to be made at 2:00 a.m. on a holiday weekend and none of the people you've designated can be reached? How do the physicians caring for you know what your wishes are? Even if your designated decision maker is able to be reached, does that person really know and understand what you would want? And even if he does, how difficult emotionally will it be for him to make the tough decisions? To take care of all these issues, you should prepare a legal document, called a living will, to make your health care wishes known.

○ STEP 5: PROTECT YOUR MINOR CHILD WITH AN EMERGENCY CHILD MEDICAL FORM

If you (or you and your spouse or partner) are away on vacation, and you leave your minor child with a friend, family member or caretaker, do they have the knowledge and authority to act in the event your child becomes ill or has an accident? In many cases they don't. The letter that many people handwrite while sitting at the kitchen table the night before they leave on vacation isn't particularly useful. If you complete and sign a form disclosing key information about your child's care, and giving instructions to any temporary caregivers, your child will be much better protected.

○ STEP 6: SIGN A WILL

Everyone knows what a will is. It is a legal document to designate where your assets should be distributed in the event of death. If you have minor children, your will should also name persons to care for your children (guardians).

○ STEP 7: CREATE A REVOCABLE LIVING TRUST

A revocable living trust is an arrangement that you make to transfer some or all of your assets to a trust during your lifetime so that on your death those assets won't be subject to the court process (called "probate") of distributing assets in accordance with your will or in accordance with state law, called "intestacy," if you die without a will.

KEY

> While the steps are the same even if you have a chronic disease, there are important differences that you need to address because of the difficulties created by your illness. Whatever the chronic illness you are living with (and many just could not be mentioned in detail in this book), the discussions throughout the rest of this book will provide you with the planning ideas and tools to address your needs.

RECONSIDERING THE 7 ESTATE PLANNING STEPS TO PROTECT SOMEONE WITH A CHRONIC ILLNESS

If you live with a chronic disease or disability, you must still take the same seven key steps to protect yourself and your assets. But there are important differences you need to address due to your medical condition.

THE FIRST STEP: COME TO TERMS WITH THE EMOTIONAL REALITIES OF YOUR HEALTH STATUS

Your comfort level in dealing with the particular issues that confront your health, future, and end-of-life decisions is vital. Your feelings will vary tremendously, based on your personal disposition, on the nature of your diagnosis, the progress of your illness, and how recently you were diagnosed. If you were recently diagnosed with a chronic illness, you may not be forthcoming about the realities of your situation and the need to plan. These hurdles have to be addressed to move forward. When selecting professionals to work with, be sure they are understanding and sensitive to your needs or the process may never get out of the starting blocks.

EXAMPLE • *Alzheimer's Disease*

Assume you were recently diagnosed with Alzheimer's disease (AD). The following is a summary of some of the key facts you face and how they impact planning. While each chronic illness has it's own complex of symptoms, and each patient has his or her own nuances, the following provides a general guideline as to the approach you should consider:

❖   The average age for the onset of AD symptoms is about 73. Given the late age of a typical diagnosis, you should aggressively and quickly address planning.

❖   The incidence and risk of AD (and other dementias) increase with age. Having an annual review meeting with all your advisers is vital to your protection. The cost of this can be controlled by carefully selecting advisers, using conference calls, and other cost-saving measures.

❖   Unlike some chronic illnesses, AD is not erratic. AD means a steady decline. While the rate of decline varies, continued loss of memory and function is certain. Thus, in contrast to multiple sclerosis, where you might have an attack (exacerbation) that remits, your AD symptoms progress downward. Again, push to get planning done as quickly as feasible after a diagnosis of AD!

❖   There is no turning back. AD, like other diseases, such as ALS and Huntington's, is irreversible. If memory loss is attributable to other physical conditions, such as vascular dementia or a stroke, medication and care may reverse the impact or prevent further deterioration. Not with AD. Current drug therapies may slow the worsening of symptoms six to twelve months, but provide no cure. Planning must be addressed while it still can be. Your estate planner must understand the time constraints.

❖   The harsh reality is that the number of years during which you will be competent are limited and death may in fact be imminent and should be planned for. Your investment and estate plans should reflect this. See Chapter 4.

❖   The duration of AD requires that planning address care, living accommodations, and financing these needs for a potentially long period. The average length of a stay in a nursing home is about 2.5 years. If you have AD and choose to stay at home, the cost of in-home care can be astronomical. For wealthier people living with AD these costs would be less of a concern, especially if long-term care insurance had been purchased to cover some portion of them. Review your financial situation with your planner as part of implementing your estate plan.

❖   Assumptions are always dangerous and the specifics of your personal situation must be addressed. Approximately 200,000 of Americans have what is referred to as younger-onset AD. Estate planners may not be familiar with this, assuming AD only effects those of much older age. You'll need to inform your advisers so they take the appropriate steps.

○ STEP 1: ORGANIZE EMERGENCY INFORMATION

Organizing emergency information is essential for everyone. However because some chronic illnesses can have cognitive symptoms, organization is now even more important! It becomes not only a useful tool for those who may help you in a future emergency, but it becomes a tool that you can use to maintain control for a longer period over your legal, tax, and financial matters, in spite of some of the disease-related difficulties you face. Thus, organizing information cannot be a static process or occasional event. Many estate and financial planning books give readers practical forms to organize lists of their financial accounts. For those struggling with a chronic illness, that type of list isn't enough. You need techniques to organize your financial records while you continue to use them, as well as to provide them to family and loved ones in a future emergency. (See Chapter 3.)

○ STEP 2: DESIGNATE A PERSON TO HANDLE FINANCIAL AND LEGAL ISSUES

If you cannot get to the bank to take care of deposits or bills, how will these important issues be tended to? If your spouse, partner, or other caretaker helps you with these tasks, what is your contingency plan if they can no longer help? If you have a chronic illness, such as Parkinson's disease, you might need help for a decade or much longer. While a healthy person your age might name one person and a successor to manage assets during some unanticipated future disability, you might be better served naming three or more alternates to assure protection over a potentially long disease course.

While everyone needs a power of attorney, you need more specific contingency planning. You must be certain that your power of attorney is "durable," which means that disability won't prevent it from being valid. Many power of attorney forms only become effective if you become disabled. But with certain chronic diseases, you may suffer an exacerbation and need help *now*, but be able to manage your affairs again in the future. Or with certain other progressive chronic diseases, such as ALS, your agent may have more advance notice to prepare before taking control of your finances. The agent you select, depending on your illness, may be required to take over sporadically and frequently over a period of time, or may not be required for several years but will eventually be full time. It is important to have this in mind when selecting an agent. You may also require some other provisions tailored to the experience of your chronic illness. Typical power of attorney forms not only don't address this, and might even include provisions that make it difficult to address your circumstances. Chapter 5 discusses these issues and special modifications you need for your power of attorney. In addition to signing a good power of attorney that is tailored to your situation, you need to take some practical steps to simplify and organize your finances.

There are additional simple steps you can take to help yourself and those you will rely on, to address the many scenarios your illness may take. One simple step could include having your agent or caretaker receive duplicate copies of your monthly bank or brokerage statement. This will help them monitor your account at no cost and with little effort. If you make a glaring mistake, or stop paying critical bills because of an exacerbation, this simple step might alert them to the situation. You might even opt to have the duplicate statement sent to someone other than the agent you named in your power of attorney, so that you have some checks and balances on anyone potentially abusing your money. These, and similar nuances in the documents and planning, can make a significant difference in protecting you and giving you peace of mind.

○ STEP 3: DESIGNATE A PERSON TO MAKE HEALTH CARE DECISIONS AND ACCESS MEDICAL RECORDS

Like anyone else, you need a health care proxy document appointing an agent to make health care decisions for you. However, most people select family members or close friends to make these decisions, without giving much thought to it. If the immediate family member or close friend you select to be your health care agent doesn't understand the implications of your disease, how can they really make decisions the way you would want? The need to communicate with your agents is vital. If your agents won't take the time to understand the implications of your illness, you may need to think about designating different people.

○ STEP 4: COMMUNICATE YOUR HEALTH CARE WISHES

Everyone should prepare a living will specifying their health care and end of life decisions. Too many people, however, simply sign short standard forms that include rather generic language stating that they don't want "heroic measures" if they are terminally ill. These simplistic forms will not suffice for you. There are many decisions that you need to communicate that hopefully have nothing to do with dying. Your care while you are alive, and especially if your condition deteriorates, is important to address. Consider donating tissue or organs for research to help other's suffering from the illness that afflicted you. Decisions as to experimental or unproven medical treatment that may allay symptoms should be addressed, and much more. You really need a living will that is tailored to your particular situation and that addresses all your potential decisions.

○ STEP 5: PROTECT YOUR MINOR CHILD WITH AN EMERGENCY CHILD MEDICAL FORM

While all parents should complete an emergency child medical form to protect their child if they are away on vacation, you may need the form to protect your child in the event that you are home but unable to physically take your child to the hospital or doctor's office. The language and wording of the form needs to be tailored to address this situation. It is important to note that if your condition has deteriorated, or might soon deteriorate, to the point where there is a good possibility that a friend or family member will have to help if your child has a medical emergency, you should provide an original signed form to your pediatrician in advance, in order to be certain that they understand it, and that they will help convince the hospitals where they are admitted to accept it.

○ STEP 6: SIGN A WILL

You need a will, just like anyone needs a will. You might wish to include a charitable bequest (gift) to an organization that helped you or a particular research facility. Even if your resources aren't large, a bequest is a great way to thank and acknowledge groups that helped you. Notifying the charity today will help them to collect the gift and enhance their record of donors, thereby encouraging more donations. If your partner or spouse writes a will, they should consider bequeathing assets to you in a trust to provide for their management and, possibly, a special type of trust that preserves those assets from being reached by nursing homes or others (a special needs trust). Most general estate planning books don't touch on this vital issue (but devote lots of time to trusts to save taxes, which may not apply to you). Your will, and that of your partner or spouse must focus on protecting you in light of the issues that your illness has or may create in the future (see Chapter 9).

○ STEP 7: CREATE AND FUND A REVOCABLE LIVING TRUST

Even though it is not a step most people think of, creating a revocable living trust may be the ideal estate planning document for you. This trust could provide the easiest and best way to allow someone to care for you and manage your assets completely when your disease renders you unable. Properly used, it can help keep you stay in control of your financial and legal decisions longer. See Chapter 10.

⚠ CAUTION

The legal and other issues, especially the sample documents and provisions presented in this book, and those provided free of charge on www.laweasy.com, are complex issues and legal documents that require the input, guidance, and assistance of a skilled estate planning attorney who is experienced and licensed in the state in which you live. The reality is that many attorneys have limited experience dealing with issues of chronic illness, so hopefully your review of the ideas and sample provisions and legal documents in this book will help guide them. The unfortunate practical reality is that although every reader of this book really should use an attorney to complete these important legal documents, it will just not happen. The ideal solution for those who cannot afford legal help is to convince an organization serving those with your chronic illness to get involved and organize an "estate planning day" with volunteer attorneys to help. You should only prepare these documents on your own as a last resort.

KEY

Every aspect of your planning—financial, estate, documents, insurance, etc.—must be tailored to address the implications of your illness.

CHAPTER SUMMARY

This chapter has provided an overview of the entire estate planning process by explaining the seven key steps you must take to protect yourself. Importantly, since every aspect of planning changes when you are living with chronic illness, each of the seven steps has been explained in a manner that applies to you.

CHAPTER 2

CHRONIC ILLNESS
ESTATE PLANNING BASICS

ESTATE PLANNING AND CHRONIC ILLNESS

IF YOU OR A LOVED ONE HAS A CHRONIC ILLNESS, estate planning takes on greater importance and requires modifications from what is typically done for those who don't have a chronic illness. Too often estate planning is viewed as merely signing "standard," or what lawyers affectionately call "boilerplate," forms. While this is dangerous for even the average person, it can be catastrophic for those with chronic illness and their loved ones. "Standard" forms just won't work for you. To help you in this process, this book will guide you through the steps you and your loved ones should evaluate. While the nuances of every chronic illness are not addressed, enough modifications and options to general planning are presented so that you can adapt the steps appropriate for you. Just like those racy car commercials that caution not to try it at home, you'll need professional help as well. This book will guide you on how to deal with an attorney and estate planner.

KEY

You need to be proactive. Don't assume that your advisers (attorney, accountant, financial planner, etc.) understand the nuances of your illness or how planning and documents need to be modified for you. You have to inform them. If you're uncomfortable discussing your illness and its potential consequences, bear in mind that if you don't make sure the people advising you really understand, you won't have the protections you or your loved ones need. However difficult, you'll benefit by being forthright, clear, and very specific.

CHRONIC ILLNESS AFFECTS ESTATE PLANNING

Even though you have a chronic illness, the same estate planning documents and planning techniques used for someone without a chronic illness, of comparable financial and other circumstances, will be used. That being said, however, every document and every aspect of planning should be tailored to address the potential impact of your chronic illness. The nature and magnitude of the changes that are necessary will depend on the chronic condition that you have, how that illness specifically impacts you, the possible range of options your disease might take, your assets, family, and other personal circumstances. If you have Parkinson's the planning may differ from what would be done if you have multiple sclerosis (MS), sickle-cell anemia, or Alzheimer's. Planning will be affected by the course that your particular disease takes. To best tailor a plan and documents to meet your needs, the nature of the specific disease that you're living with needs to be addressed. Helping you do just that is a key goal of this book.

KEY

> Your experience with chronic disease is unique to you. Thus, while estate planning should consider the potential impact of your particular illness, it should be tailored to address your personal experience and the likely trajectory that your illness will take.

EXAMPLE • *Multiple Sclerosis*

To illustrate planning modifications, assume that you were recently diagnosed with MS. The changes to the documentation and planning will be based on an understanding of what MS is, how it affects you now, and how it will likely affect you in the future. MS is a neurological disorder of the central nervous system. MS is characterized by an inflammatory process that results in the destruction of the myelin sheaths that surround and insulate axons (nerve fibers), and causes damage to those axons. These lesions are typically detected in an MRI as plaques. In progressive forms of MS, the cells that create new myelin, called oligodendrocytes, are also destroyed. This precludes repair of destroyed myelin (remyelination) making improvement in your condition unlikely absent new medical discoveries. Identifying the type of MS you have, and the disease course of that category, and then explaining it in understandable English to your estate planners is essential since planning will differ.

❖   **BENIGN:** If you have a benign form of MS, there is likely to be limited impact on planning, but modifications should occur if the MS worsens. If a negative change in the prognosis occurs, more substantial planning modifications, as discussed below, should be addressed. Many neurologists question the existence of a benign form of MS. Thus, anyone with a diagnosis of MS might be best served by taking more formal steps to address it in their planning.

❖   **RELAPSING/REMITTING:** If you have a form of relapsing MS, the disease is characterized by acute attacks (exacerbations) followed by remissions. An attack can last for a short duration or remain for days or even several weeks. It might be characterized by symptoms similar to a stroke involving severe visual, motor and sensory problems. Eighty-five percent of those with MS begin with this subtype. The occurrence of exacerbations differentiates planning for clients with MS from planning for clients with other chronic illnesses, such as Alzheimer's and Parkinson's. Months or years can pass between attacks. Following an attack, you may recover from most or all of the disabilities suffered during the attack. Only 10 percent of those with MS will gain all function back when an attack subsides. This all needs to be addressed in the planning process. You may choose to use a limited or special power of attorney to enable someone to handle routine financial matters during these periods, but not to make major financial decisions that you will be able to deal with in short order (Chapter 5). You may choose to rely on a HIPAA release (Chapter 6) rather than abrogating medical decision making during these periods to an agent under a health care proxy (Chapter 7).

❖   **SECONDARY PROGRESSIVE:** In secondary progressive, primary progressive, or progressive relapsing MS, the disease worsens progressively over time. This subtype of MS is most similar to ALS, in which speech and motor abilities become progressively worse over time. This prognosis may require more significant planning for disability. Unfortunately, about 50 percent of those that begin with relapsing-remitting MS (above) advance to secondary-progressive within ten years of their initial diagnosis. With secondary-progressive MS full recovery does not occur after an attack. The disease progression appears steplike. An attack is followed by partial or even no recovery. The next attack is again followed by only partial or no recovery. Each attack brings a higher degree of neurological impairment.

❖ **PROGRESSIVE RELAPSING:** In a small number of MS patients, the disease is characterized by continued progression, even between attacks. This contrasts unfavorably to relapsing-remitting MS, in which people tend to remain stable between attacks.

❖ **PRIMARY PROGRESSIVE:** In about 10 percent of MS patients, the disease worsens progressively, without the distinct exacerbations that accompany other forms of MS. Planning for this type of MS is thus more akin to clients with Parkinson's or Alzheimer's than to planning for the majority of those with MS.

In addition to these more significant implications, MS can result in extreme fatigue, cognitive dysfunction of varying degrees, and physical impairment. (Not all chronic illnesses lead to both physical and cognitive dysfunction. For example, AD is primarily cognitive, while ALS has no cognitive effects at all.) The course of MS (like several other chronic illnesses) is unpredictable; the effects range from mild to devastating. Such a diagnosis affects every aspect of your estate and financial planning. Some of the modifications are minor, some significant. But in all events, some special planning steps should be implemented immediately. Other planning modifications can be viewed as more long-term goals.

CAUTION TO PROFESSIONAL ADVISERS

Misconceptions about chronic illness are common, and very dangerous to those living with chronic illness and their loved ones. Don't assume that your advisers understand. Make a point of explaining and educating. Some major misconceptions include:

❖ *Chronic illness is uncommon.* The reality is that many millions of people are affected. It is not rare or unusual.

❖ *Planning is the same.* False. Henry Ford joked that you could have the Model T in any color—as long as it was black. Don't let a planner convince you of the same choice. There are tremendous variations and nuances. Don't let your planner make assumptions. Inform them of your current situation and the likely future consequences.

❖ *Invest short term and use special needs trusts.* These do not hold true for everyone with a chronic disease or disability. Investigate all options.

EXAMPLE • *Alzheimer's Disease*

Alzheimer's disease (AD) affects every aspect of your life. Dementia is a certainty and life longevity is reduced. AD is surprisingly common so its planning implications need to be taken seriously. More than five million people in the United States have AD. AD also has a dramatic impact on the caregivers and immediate family. Both planning and document drafting, for you and your loved ones, must be modified.

CHRONICALLY ILL FAMILY MEMBER
INCAPABLE OF SIGNING DOCUMENTS

If your loved one is living with a chronic illness and they put off planning too long, they may no longer have the ability to sign documents or take informed planning steps. In such situations, you'll be reading this book instead of them. Their inability doesn't mean the inability to help. It just limits the options and demands different approaches. If, for example, your parent has AD and their disease has progressed too far for them to sign a will or other documents, planning must take on a different perspective. Some of these steps are summarized below:

❖ Carefully confirm the mental status of your loved one. It may still be feasible to sign a will even though he or she does not have sufficient contractual capacity to sign a trust or other contractual document.

❖ Determine in consultation with your loved one's caregiver and medical providers if he or she has periods when cognition may be greater. For example, for someone with moderate AD, confusion is common, and it often worsens at night. It may be worthwhile to evaluate competency early in the day when confusion is less pronounced. A client with Huntington's disease may have difficulty concentrating, or have mood swings. Many of the chronic illnesses trigger depression. It may be possible for a loved one with significant cognitive issues to have periods when they are quite lucid. If you have to use this approach, be certain to hire an experienced estate attorney to make certain that all the appropriate legal formalities of signing a document during a period of lucidity are addressed.

❖   In order to assist your loved one, you will need access to medical records. Scour existing legal documents and inquire of his or her attending physician and neurologist whether documents authorizing the release of private health information (PHI) were signed. These are necessary in most circumstances to access a loved one's medical records as a result of HIPAA laws, which are discussed in Chapter 6.

❖   Inventory all assets and liabilities. Pay particular attention to the exact manner in which ownership is worded ("title") and whether beneficiary designation forms (indicating who inherits the asset on death) exist and who is listed.

❖   Coordinate estate needs with the patient's financial planner, including addressing the financial contribution of various insurance policies. It may be possible, using the title to certain assets, beneficiary designations, and the ability of well family members and others listed to decline benefit from those assets (in legal jargon: "disclaim" or "renounce"), in order to direct those assets as desired even in the absence of your loved one's ability to sign a new will.

❖   Obtain, read, and analyze all existing estate planning documents with an estate attorney. Determine what options may be utilized in the current situation to better help your loved one. If there is no valid will, evaluate the impact of the state's intestacy laws on the situation. These rules say who should inherit assets when there is no will. If your loved one had signed a durable power of attorney (see Chapter 5) you may want the person named in that document (the "agent") to modify beneficiary designations and title to assets to affect the desired results.

❖   Evaluate the merits of seeking a court appointed guardianship. For example, your loved one may have a substantial taxable estate and the only flexibility under existing estate planning documents executed prior to his or her becoming incompetent are limited to making annual gifts up to the annual gift exclusion amount ($13,000 that can be given away to any number of people without a gift tax consequence under 2009 law). That limit will hardly make a dent in the taxable estate. Consider whether the powers permit establishing and contributing to a family limited partnership or other entity that may discount values (and the risks of that type of planning). Evaluate the potential for a court conferring on a guardian the right to make more extensive estate planning steps.

For the rest of this book it will generally be assumed that "you" are the reader and the person living with chronic illness, although some additional planning ideas for your loved ones will be noted, primarily in Chapter 12.

KEY

> ⚷ **It is your responsibility to do as Dr. Phil always recommends: "Get real" and lay the cards on the table so your planners can help you instead of relying on their preconceived notions of what your situation might be. If you are reading this book for a family member living with chronic illness, the reality is that many people struggle to come to terms with what their current condition is and how it may impact them in the future. If you really care about this person, you have to guide, encourage, and help. This is especially important if your loved one suffers from illness-related depression or apathy.**

HOW CHRONIC ILLNESSES AFFECT ESTATE PLANNING

There are a host of ways your chronic illness makes the estate planning process different.

COMMUNICATE WITH YOUR ATTORNEY AND OTHER ADVISERS

Here are some discussion points to prepare for your estate planner:

❖ What illness do you have? What category or type of that illness do you have, and what does that distinction mean to your current situation and likely future situations? Each category may have different planning implications.

❖ Is your course of the disease mild, moderate or severe? What is your current state of disability and how rapidly is it expected to progress? These factors will help indicate time frames for planning, whether a trust should be used, etc. There are significant differences between various chronic illnesses. MS is not a fatal disease and progresses slowly for many people. ALS, in contrast, usually progresses rapidly and can result in death from respiratory failure within three to five years. There are exceptions, however. The well-known physicist Stephen Hawking, for example, has had

ALS for 30 years. Alzheimer's will result in dementia and death but over a longer period then ALS. The time horizons differ, and these differences are significant to planning.

❖   When were you diagnosed? For some illnesses, the older you are when symptoms first appeared, the poorer your diagnosis. Conversely, the earlier the age at which the disease appears, the slower the progression.

❖   Are you having any cognitive impairment currently, and, if so, to what extent? There maybe no correlation between visible physical impairment and cognitive impairment. You must therefore explicitly explore these issues with your attorney.

❖   Arrange to bring a clarifying letter from your attending physician and/or neurologist to address the above issues for your attorney.

EXAMPLE • *Parkinson's Disease*

You were recently diagnosed with Parkinson's disease (PD). You should explain to your attorney that PD is a chronic, progressive incurable neurological

KEY

> ⚷   **You need to communicate details about your condition to your estate planner and other advisers.**

disorder that can impact both physical and mental functioning. However, you should also explain that the symptoms of PD can vary greatly from person to person, and even within an individual. Variation will occur over time, sometimes from hour to hour in more advanced disease stages and depends on your medication schedule. The cause of PD is very different in people.

CHOOSING PEOPLE (FIDUCIARIES) YOU CAN RELY ON

When most people choose an executor (the person to manage their affairs when they die) or a health care agent (the person to make medical decisions if they can't), it's often a theoretical exercise. They generally don't believe death or serious medical decisions are imminent (tempting fate is a favorite past time for most people who are "fine"). For you, the decisions are real, important, difficult, and depending on the illness you are contending with, imminent. This makes these appointments all important to your planning.

Almost every legal document discussed in this book is dependent upon a person you designate carrying out your wishes as set forth in the document. The best health care proxy isn't worth much if the person you select to make medical decisions cannot do it, or lacks the knowledge or sensitivity (or both!) that you anticipated.

Most people select immediate family members as agents. However, everyone living with a chronic illness has a very different experience of how their loved ones react to their illness. Bonnie, in the introduction, has an estranged brother who has never come through. Sadly many people abandon a spouse diagnosed with a chronic illness (so much for the vow of "for better or worse…in sickness or health"). Fortunately for some, family and friends become foundations of unwavering support after the diagnosis. Others are unable to deal with the circumstances and are unsupportive; some may virtually disappear from your life because of their discomfort facing your diagnosis or other trivial reasons or perceived slights. These reactions, whichever direction they take, will give you invaluable insight into which people to name as fiduciaries and which to avoid.

Many chronic illnesses are enigmatic. So much remains unknown about the manner in which many of these illnesses affect people. Many people living with ulcerative colitis, multiple sclerosis, and certain other chronic illnesses or neurological diseases seem "fine" on the surface, so another common reaction for some family and loved ones is to continue on "business as usual," not believing, understanding, or accepting the significant challenges you might face. In these cases, it may be more difficult for you to determine the appropriateness of naming these people as your fiduciaries. A frank and detailed discussion is probably advisable.

The bottom line is that you should not assume that the usual cast of characters should automatically be named to serve as your fiduciaries. Don't let your attorney lead the conversation by suggesting the usual relationships to serve in these capacities if they are not really appropriate for you. Your attorney will have no way of knowing reactions of your family and loved ones without your input. Discuss your concerns and options. If you are newly diagnosed, you should honestly reevaluate who you designated as fiduciaries in your existing documents in light of how these presumably important people have reacted since your diagnosis.

Because there is no cure for most chronic illnesses, and for most your condition will worsen, you have a much greater probability of having to rely on your fiduciaries in vital ways and over a longer time period. It is particularly important for you to select fiduciaries based on what the prospective fiduciaries have demonstrated they can do to assist you, not out of familial obligation. This is no time for decisions motivated by guilt or friendship.

Careful consideration should be given to naming an institutional cotrustee to ensure the fiduciary long-term viability. This lessens the long-term and potentially significant administrative burdens on a friend or family member who might otherwise have served alone as fiduciary. Don't dismiss naming a bank or trust company because of rumors you've heard about their poor performance or lack of sensitivity. These complaints are incorrect. The real "problem" with institutional trustees that most people have is exactly the reason you should favor an institution. Institutional trustees operate "by the book." What the legal documents provide for is exactly what they are going to do. In contrast, when trusty Uncle Joe is serving as a trustee, he *might* just do whatever is asked of him. If you are living with a chronic illness, especially one that will eventually impact your cognitive abilities to a degree that you will become dependent on your fiduciaries, you want the integrity and formality of an institutional trustee that will adhere to your wishes. There is no better way to protect yourself. Boilerplate cheap internet documents make great commercials, but not much more. Tailored documents with an institutional trustee are your best assurance. Even a step better is to name a trusted family member, friend or loved one, to serve together with the institution (when multiple trustees serve they are called "cotrustees"). Bear in mind that institutions will serve as executors (to administer your estate), and as trustees (to administer trusts you set up). They cannot serve as agents under your power of attorney (Chapter 5) or health care proxy (Chapter 7).

KEY

> The best way to avoid perceived complaints that people have about institutions is to take the time to carefully tailor your estate planning documents to your needs and wishes.

Selecting fiduciaries if you have a chronic illness has some other nuances to consider:

❖   If you are living with ulcerative colitis, Crohn's disease, pancreatitis, or most types of MS, the disease is characterized by unpredictable attacks, lasting for days or weeks. The on–off use of an agent requires fast reaction for short durations with no notice. The agent selected under a power of attorney or health proxy must be appropriate to this unique circumstance. Preparing the agent in advance is also important.

❖   If you have a steadily deteriorating chronic illness, Alzheimer's, Parkinson's, ALS, Huntington's or other illnesses, an agent under a durable power or a successor trustee under a living trust might have advanced notice of the pending need to serve as your condition worsens and in advance of taking control of your affairs. This might make an agent who lives further away more feasible than for the illnesses described above.

❖   Often agents are selected based on their understanding of your major objectives and wishes. However, since you are living with a chronic illness, the focus is different. Your agent under your durable power of attorney, or a successor trustee under a living trust, should be able and willing to handle routine financial and legal details over a long period, not just a few big decisions. Depending on your illness, you may have the mental presence to make major decisions, even if those decisions have to wait for an exacerbation to subside. This is substantially different than the focus for other chronic neurological disorders where significant cognitive impairment is likely (such as Alzheimer's). These factors may affect who you select as an agent. For example, if you have MS and are unlikely to have significant cognitive impairment, you might be more comfortable naming a friend as cotrustee of a living trust with you since you can monitor their activities. On the other hand, if you have a chronic illness that will assuredly result in dementia, such as Alzheimer's disease (AD), you might prefer the security of naming a major independent financial institution to ensure that no liberties are taking with your assets.

❖   If you don't face significant cognitive impairment, you might wish to retain a power to replace trustees even if you give up the role of trustee for yourself because of the strain it causes you. For more sophisticated planning, you might use a third party, such as a trust protector, to provide a check and balance on the trustees.

EXAMPLE • *Huntington's Disease*

Huntington's disease is a rare, inherited, progressive, degenerative disorder. Huntington's exhibits itself in jerky, uncontrolled movements, severe problems with balance and coordination, and slow movement as well as dementia and some behavioral changes. The progression of Huntington's is so strong that you will eventually require full-time care and become mentally incompetent until death. A person with Huntington's will need to specifically detail your end-of-life decisions and wishes. You need to be sure that agents you name under your health care proxy understand what your future holds and that they have the emotional ability to truly carry out your wishes. You might consider establishing a revocable living trust with an institution as the sole trustee or cotrustee to ensure that your assets are managed as you wish for the rest of your life, especially when you will not be able to make decisions. Depending on the likely disease course, you may name a loved one as cotrustee with the institution from the initial formation of your trust. Keep in mind, that with this illness a blood relative may also develop the disease so that you and the relative may both be disabled. So pick your trustee carefully. On your death, you may no longer need the services of the institutional trustee, even if your estate is paid into trusts (e.g., for your children or nieces and nephews). This illustrates an important point of flexibility. You can provide for changes in who will serve as trustee for different phases of your planning.

EXAMPLE • *ALS (Lou Gehrig's Disease)*

ALS is a progressive neurodegenerative disease that affects the neurons that control muscle movement. Initially a patient with ALS will experience muscle twitching, cramping and weakness, but as the disease progresses, he will eventually require a permanent ventilator to assist with breathing. Most people with ALS will not experience significant cognitive symptoms. These factors might suggest the use of a revocable living trust with an institution serving as cotrustee with you. This will enable you to retain as much control over major decisions as possible, while relegating all administrative matters to a skilled institution.

CHRONIC ILLNESS AFFECTS THE TIMING OF PLANNING

Chronic illness affects the time horizon you have to make decisions and implement planning. It's important to clearly inform your attorney and other advisers of the time line of your illness and, most importantly, of how that illness affects you. Timing can be critical to estate planning, and too many advisers, unless they've been personally touched by chronic illness, may not understand the implications. Worse yet, they might tend to make the same erroneous assumptions most people do, and lump all chronic illnesses together as if they all have the same symptoms and implications.

EXAMPLE • *Parkinson's Disease*

Parkinson's disease (PD) is not rare; about one percent of all those over age 65 are diagnosed with it. The average age at onset for PD is about 60, but it can also affect people under the age of 40 (referred to as young onset PD, or YOPD). Your documents and planning should all be modified to reflect the implications of PD. At the outset, PD can be managed well enough with medications and lifestyle changes so that you might live a relatively unaffected life for years, even decades. But because PD is in all cases a progressive illness, symptoms will worsen over time. Thus, while planning may not need to be addressed on an urgent basis when you are initially diagnosed, the likelihood of progression means it should not be put off for too long. Don't use this time period to delay planning. Use it as an opportunity. Engage in planning as soon as feasible after your diagnosis. Then use the time remaining to tailor and modify your planning. Update your documents, as the circumstances of your diagnosis become clearer and as your feelings and wishes evolve. Because PD progresses over many years, there will likely be refinements, if not changes, as you reevaluate your feelings and wishes over time.

    PD is also a chronic illness, in contrast to an acute illness. The symptoms are permanent and will continue. Annual reviews, after initial documents and planning are completed, to ensure adequtey, are advisable. This is important since you will not be able to judge when you become incapable of making decisions.

CHRONIC ILLNESS AFFECTS THE ECONOMICS OF PLANNING

How does the disease course of your chronic illness affect the economics of your estate planning? Most advisers erroneously assume that everyone with a chronic illness has limited resources, needs to focus investment planning on liquidity and minimum risk, and should have a non-springing power of attorney, etc. Some chronic illnesses strike early, truncating even the most lucrative of careers. Others, such as Parkinson's and Alzheimer's, tend to strike at later ages (the young onset versions being an exception). Even some diseases that are diagnosed at an earlier age, such as multiple sclerosis, allow somewhat normal lives, until becoming more severe at a later age. This is important, because an initial diagnosis much later in life may have afforded you the opportunity to earn and save assets through a normal retirement age. Generalizations are dangerous. You must make sure to inform your advisers of your specific circumstances and be sure they plan accordingly. See the discussion in Chapter 12 concerning investment planning for those living with chronic illness.

EXAMPLE • *Parkinson's Disease*

Because PD tends to occur primarily after age 60, and progresses over time, many PD patients will have had a relatively unimpeded career and hence have estate tax and other planning concerns similar to people without a chronic illness. The costs of care can be significant, and this too has to be factored into the planning. Modifying your home to make it safer to avoid falls, redecorating, perhaps even adding on a room for a caretaker, might all warrant factoring into your planning. There could also be substantial differences in the type of insurance coverages and other benefits you may have from your employment. Perhaps you purchased long-term care coverage before your diagnosis, maybe you were not that fortunate. The differences between various people with PD can be significant. Again, you must explain how your PD affects you to your advisers. Don't assume that they will understand these nuances.

EXAMPLE • *Young Onset Chronic Disease*

Young onset Parkinson's disease has been diagnosed at ages as early as 30. For all YOPD patients, the disease will have a negative impact on their career and savings. A small percentage of those with Alzheimer's disease (AD) are diagnosed in their fifties, or perhaps earlier (young onset AD). But even for these people, there are significant exceptions. There are those with young onset disease that have already had significant financial success. Michael J. Fox might be one of the most famous and outspoken, but he is not the only one. If your attorney assumes that all those living with young onset variations of chronic illness have similar circumstances, the planning you receive could be quite the opposite of what is appropriate for you.

A NOTE TO FAMILY AND CARETAKERS

If your loved one has a chronic illness your role and importance in their estate planning will differ, often markedly, from that of a spouse, partner, or loved one for someone who does not face the same challenges. Your role in serving as a catalyst to get their estate and financial planning process moving, may be the most important role you serve.

EXAMPLE • *Alzheimer's Disease*

Apathy can affect many people with a chronic illness. It is vital for you, if your loved one has Alzheimer's, to encourage, even push, them to complete planning before the disease progresses to the point of making it impossible to implement planning. Dementia is not a possibility if your loved one has AD, it is a certainty. Yet the apathy AD creates may make your loved one act in the opposite manner of what all logic and caution would indicate. If your loved one is not pursuing the appropriate planning with sufficient earnest, encourage them to move forward. Enlist their neurologist, attorney, and others to support your efforts to get them to address planning.

Those with AD commonly suffer from language problems (aphasia). As your loved one with AD struggles to identify the correct term or phrase to use in conversation, his or her ability to understand an attorney's comments, and to read documents (e.g., to understand a power of attorney and other documents) all deteriorate. This decline will set a time frame, and perhaps urgency, to completing more sophisticated planning quickly.

Personality changes are a common symptom of AD. A loved one with AD might become delusional and/or suspicious. These changes may have the AD loved one stop trusting you, family members, and others named as fiduciaries. A power of attorney, revocable trust or other document could be revoked when in fact it should have been retained as a protection against the very issues leading the person with AD to inappropriately revoke it.

Isolation can occur as your loved one with AD becomes embarrassed over his or her inability to communicate, maintain personal hygiene, etc.

Aggressiveness, anxiety and other symptoms can also occur. To protect and help them it is essential that you guide them to complete the necessary planning, as soon as feasible. Perhaps, with your intimate knowledge of your loved ones feelings, you can specifically address some of these impediments to them proceeding with planning.

PREPARE FOR YOUR FIRST MEETING WITH YOUR ESTATE PLANNER

When you prepare for your first meeting with your estate planner, there are some basics steps you can take to make the meeting go more smoothly, productively, and quickly. This will translate into a better result, greater likelihood of achieving your goals, and lower costs (to the extent that your attorney and other planners bill hourly).

❖   *Balance sheet.* Prepare a balance sheet listing your assets (things you own) by category and how they are owned. If feasible, attach copies of the relevant documents to back up the numbers on the balance sheet (e.g., a brokerage statement, deed, etc.). For many of the goals of estate planning it is the "big picture" that must be understood. The balance sheet is really a snapshot, a mile-high picture, at a point in time of what you own and what you owe.

❖   *Family tree.* An attorney will need a summary of all family members, regardless of your feelings toward them. At a minimum, this should include parents, siblings, children, grandchildren. If anyone is deceased, divorced, has a health issue, is not a United States citizen, indicate this. Also, provide each person's full legal name, nickname if commonly used, Social Security number, address, and age. "Family" is defined differently for everyone. If there are people whom you consider your family, even if they don't follow the pattern of the Cleaver family, list them and explain their relationship. Most estate planning books continue to be written as if June and Ward Cleaver are the prototype American family! The key to avoid the estate problems many people have is to make sure that you take the time to carefully communicate your background information and wishes.

❖   *List of trustees, agents and other fiduciaries.* If you can provide a list of a minimum of one fiduciary and at least two alternates (successors) for each of the estate planning documents discussed in this book, you'll save considerable time. Provide the persons full legal name, nickname if commonly used, address and age. You might want to note why you have named this particular person, and whether you have any concerns about naming them. This will put your questions squarely on the table for your attorney to address with you quickly and efficiently.

❖   List of intended donees and beneficiaries. Who should inherit? Who should receive gifts? If you are leaving assets unequally (e.g., favoring a child who has been your caretaker) indicate why the difference.

Since you have a chronic illness, you need to prepare additional information and materials for your planner. Having these ready to prepare and present at your first meeting will also save time and money, and better assure that your goals are met.

❖   What chronic illness do you have? Be specific, primary-progressive multiple sclerosis is more informative then merely saying MS. Be prepared to explain any nuances.

❖   What are the current symptoms of your illness?

❖   What is your age? How does age impact your condition? For example, dementia tends to affect those with PD over age 70 more than younger people living with PD.

❖   What insurance coverage do you have?

❖   What other health issues do you have? You need to make sure your estate planner understands the potential course of your illness and your general health since other health issues can accompany your chronic illness, exacerbate its impact, and accelerate the progression of problems. For example, many people living with PD also have cardiovascular issues, high blood pressure, and other ailments that may independently cause dementia (called "secondary dementia") or exacerbate your PD dementia.

❖   Are you presently having any cognitive impairment, and if so, to what extent? Your caregiver or possibly your neurologist may need to supply the answer to this question. Your attorney will have to determine whether an independent report from your neurologist and perhaps internist (as to other health issues) should be obtained and what those reports should address. If you will be seeing your physicians prior to your estate planner, obtaining a letter that describes your situation and especially concludes that you have the mental capacity to engage in planning and sign complex legal documents will be quite useful. Even if a more detailed letter is later requested by your attorney (e.g., before you consummate a complex and technical estate planning transaction), the initial letter will be quite valuable to support the conclusions of competency in the later letter. See Chapter 4.

❖   Many chronic illnesses are enigmatic and variable in nature. You may lack sufficient technical understanding of your own condition and prognosis, or emotions may make it too difficult for you to relate these points. Consider requesting a clarifying letter from your attending neurologist to address these matters, as well as the competency issue noted above. Since each person's chronic disease progresses in its own unique manner, some detailed understanding is important to assess the urgency of planning. This information will be different then the focus of the competency report noted above.

❖   Will you need caretaker assistance? When? What plans have been made to address this?

❖   If you have a care plan prepared by a social worker, geriatric consultant, or other specialist, bring a copy as this could be a very informative road map for your estate planner.

INFORM YOUR ESTATE PLANNER HOW YOUR CHRONIC ILLNESS AFFECTS YOUR INTERACTIONS WITH THEM

You should inform your attorney and other advisers of what steps they need to take to modify their practices to accommodate your needs. Letting them know in advance will make the process more comfortable for all. Are there certain times of day—perhaps correlated to the impact of your medication or when your symptoms are the least pronounced—that it would be preferable to schedule appointments and conference calls? While this book explores a number of illnesses, space limitations prevent a detailed discussion of each. So be certain to explain your situation to your planners

The main physical symptoms of PD that affect most people, even early in the disease, include rigidity, tremor, bradykinesia, or slowed movement, and akinesia, the inability to move spontaneously, which can make it difficult for someone with PD to begin, or continue, an action. A common impact of this is in their facial expressions. Tell your attorney not to assume that a blank facial expression indicates that you are not paying attention or following a discussion, or that you have a significant cognitive impairment. The reality may be the opposite of all of these assumed implications. Rigidity causes stiffness, mainly of the arms or legs. Tremors can be mild or severe, intermittent or constant, and most commonly affect the hands. All of these symptoms contribute to making writing a particularly difficult task. This can have a significant impact on your ability to sign legal documents. Ways to address this include eliminating unnecessary signatures or initials. For example, some attorneys as a matter of practice have clients sign every page of a will with their full signature. Other attorneys only have each page initialed. Unless there is a legal requirement to have every page signed, using initials will make the process less tedious, difficult, and time consuming.

❖   As your PD progresses, balance and walking may also be affected. In particular, some people will "freeze" while trying to walk through a doorway or when approaching a chair to sit down. Their legs will simply not do what they want them to do. Your advisers might wish to move tripping hazards or take other modest precautions for you.

❖   Other symptoms of PD may include dysarthria (slurred speech) and hypophonia (very soft speech). This can make it difficult to understand what you are saying and can be frustrating for both you as the speaker and your attorney as the listener. Turning up the volume on a telephone, using a land phone line rather than a cellular phone, using the actual phone and not a speaker phone, can often help. In many cases, if your attorney simply takes the time and exercises the patience to focus, he or she will be able to understand you. If, however, an answer to an important question is not understood, you should and must repeat yourself to your attorney until he or she does understand your reply. Whatever discomfort or frustration you or your attorney may have, this pales by comparison to the damage that might be done if your attorney does not properly understand your wishes. For meetings, and even phone calls, it might be possible to have a friend, family member or even caretaker who is familiar with your voice, participate and repeat your comments. Be careful however, as it may be inadvisable to have a caretaker, or even certain family members, hear discussions about your assets and bequests.

❖   Some people living with PD can experience drooling, which can be embarrassing. If you do, bring extra tissues to the meeting, but explaining these symptoms to your advisers in advance will make it easier for everyone.

❖   The main neuro-symptoms of PD include depression, anxiety, cognitive problems, and apathy. Some living with PD may also experience psychiatric side effects from medications used to treat their PD, namely psychosis (delusions or hallucinations) or confusion. You may personally experience none, some, or all of these problems. This is why informing your attorney about your specific situation, rather than leaving them to rely on generalizations about PD (or worse yet, just ignoring it all and not making any effort to understand) will undermine your ability to be best served by your advisers.

❖   Many people living with PD exhibit bradyphrenia, or a slowing down of their thought processes. It can take longer for them to respond to a question even when they understand it perfectly well. If bradyphrenia affects you, explain this to your advisers so that they will understand that they need to give you more time to respond, that no response doesn't mean your consent to a statement made (it might just mean you're still trying to get the answer out). Inform your attorney that the impact of bradyphrenia has no implication to your competency. Explain that patience is essential and that they should allot more time for your meetings. If an introductory meeting typically receives a two-hour allotment on your attorney's calendar system, suggest that they allow for three hours for you to address your PD symptoms.

❖   Older people and those with advancing disease appear to be at particular risk for cognitive problems. Even early on, many people have subtle cognitive difficulties that may affect their ability to concentrate, multitask, and plan effectively. These are sometimes referred to as "executive" functions. Suggest that your attorney focus meetings and discussions on a limited number of issues at a time, that he or she organize the issues in logical or natural sequence to facilitate discussions, making it easier for your participation.

❖   As your PD progresses, you may develop frank dementia and may be disoriented to place, date, or time. At this stage, you may lack sufficient judgment to effectively make legal decisions. However, for many with PD, their ability to make major decisions will never be completely undermined. A more detailed discussion about the impact of cognitive impairment on estate planning and suggestions for dealing with it is presented in Chapter 4. You may be perfectly competent to make decisions at one point in your representation by an estate planner, but you may not be at a later point. If significant transactions are to be engaged in, e.g., a large complex note sale transaction to a defective grantor dynasty trust, counsel should endeavor to corroborate that at that time of your signing documents you were in fact capable of understanding the transaction. An issue for your attorney may be determining and documenting your competency, and determining when the cognitive impact of PD has reached a point on the continuum that a particular level of planning might be inappropriate to consummate.

❖   Motor fluctuations are phenomena of PD and tend to be particularly problematic in YOPD. At first, PD medications work very well and symptoms tend to be relatively constant throughout the day. However, as the disease progresses, you may experience a "wearing off" of their medications with a return of your PD symptoms as they are approaching the time of their next dose. Inform your attorney that you need to take your medications on time. Request that water be made available, and that your meeting pause, to allow you to take your medications. A simple solution is for your advisers to have a decanter of water and glasses on hand so that you can help yourself comfortably whenever necessary. It is also advisable to arrange the timing of your meetings to best fit your medication/symptom cycle.

❖   You might experience periods of extremely poor mobility ("off" periods) and good mobility ("on" periods). "On" periods can be associated with excessive, involuntary movements (dyskinesia). Dyskinesias can manifest as subtle wiggling movements or more severe flailing movements of the head, body, arms, or legs. Subtle movements might give you the appearance of being nervous or restless when, in fact, you are not. Severe dyskinesia can make performing some tasks, like writing, very difficult. Dyskinesia (unless severe) may alarm others more than it bothers you. However, if your advisers are not familiar with this symptom, explaining it in advance is advisable. (Several of the symptoms described in this example are not unique to PD. For example, motor fluctuations are apparent in ALS and Huntington's patients, while dyskinesia occurs as a side effect of some medications.)

EXAMPLE • *Larger Adviser Role*

What role should your attorney and other advisers play? In most instances, advisors work directly with their client. However, depending on your symptoms and especially as your illness progresses, there may be times when your advisers could help you most by communicating with your fiduciaries (agent under a power of attorney) and loved ones directly. To facilitate this, specific steps to authorize communication with others must be taken. If your illness will eventually result in dementia or substantial incapacity, this point should be addressed when you are first deciding which advisers to retain. You should focus on experienced practitioners who won't abuse the authority you are giving them, and who are conscientious enough not to neglect the responsibility you are delegating. As no surprise, the internet and computer-prepared legal forms not only won't address this nuance, but they cannot provide this degree of help. Similarly, your family attorney who is nearly 80 years old, is not an ideal candidate.

For attorneys, reaching out to family members if not authorized to do so by their client may constitute a violation of attorney ethics so advanced preparation is required. Consider including an "authorization to communicate" in the retainer agreement and even in specific estate planning documents (e.g., a durable power of attorney).

Sample Provision

I expressly authorize [ATTORNEY NAME] to communicate with the agent named under my durable power of attorney, health care proxy, as well as my wealth manager [ADVISOR NAME], and my certified public accountant [CPA NAME]. Collectively my agent and accountant named herein are referred to as "Recipients." I understand that [ATTORNEY NAME] will have to exercise judgment as to what communication is appropriate in the circumstances. Therefore, I authorize [ATTORNEY NAME] in her sole discretion to communicate, or not communicate, with any person named as a Recipient, or any successor or alternate to them designated in the same document appointing a Recipient. I understand and agree that this authorization may constitute an express waiver of the attorney-client privilege that I have with [ATTORNEY NAME]. I, on behalf of myself and my estate, successors and assigns, hold [ATTORNEY NAME] harmless from the exercise or nonexercise of this power.

Similar steps may be advisable to take with your other advisers. For example, you may sign a HIPAA release that permits your insurance consultant to speak with your agent or others. The investment policy statement (IPS) you sign with your wealth manager (the document that establishes the manner in which your funds will be invested) might be modified to expressly authorize your wealth manager's communication with your financial agent

IF YOU CAN'T AFFORD AN ESTATE PLANNER

Whether your resources are very limited or your estate substantial, this book will give you guidance on how to make sure your planning and documents are crafted to address the special circumstances your chronic illness creates, and to help you minimize legal and other professional fees. However, if you don't have sufficient funds to spend, how can you obtain the benefits of the ideas and sample provisions contained in this book? If you're doing it alone using a computer program for documents, you can modify those documents to reflect the information, ideas, and sample provisions and forms in this book and those provided on www.laweasy.com. However, there is never a substitute for the judgment of an experienced estate planning attorney. One approach is for the organizations serving people with your particular chronic illness to set up programs with volunteer attorneys and other planners to help those who cannot afford legal help to get it.

✔ **GET INVOLVED** If an association you're involved with heeds the call to establish these programs, or "estate planning days," in your area you might be able to accomplish all of this at little or no cost. There are myriad wonderful organizations each typically dedicated to aiding those suffering with a particular chronic illness, raising funds for research and programming, etc. If each of those organizations would organize an estate planning day on the local chapter level, a much better level of help can be provided. For those suffering with a similar chronic illness and income and net worth levels below certain thresholds, there should be substantial similarities in many of the documents and planning steps to make an estate planning day organized by a particular organization feasible to run.

WHAT THIS BOOK DOESN'T COVER

This book does not address a number of issues that receive much media attention, and which are included in most estate planning books. This is done intentionally, so read on.

PROBATE

This book doesn't really address probate avoidance to a great extent. Probate is the process by which an estate is settled after someone dies. Too often, avoiding probate becomes the focus of an entire estate plan. While there can be benefits of avoiding probate, sometimes substantial ones, that goal should never be the focus of your estate plan. The primary goal of your estate plan (or if you are a Star Trek fan, the "Prime Directive") is to take care of *you*. Probate only occurs when you die. Further, if you own assets jointly with your spouse, partner, or other intended beneficiaries (see Chapter 3) you'll avoid probate. Also, many if not most of your assets may never be subject to probate anyway because they pass to heirs without the formal probate process (e.g., retirement assets and insurance pass by beneficiary designations, not probate). Probate should just not be the focus of your planning. If your estate is modest enough for you to use the forms in this book (say under $500,000) probate will in most cases not be that big of a deal. Most importantly, planning to minimize probate is no different for someone with a chronic illness and anyone else, so there are few new planning ideas to be provided. Finally, a tremendously powerful tool to protect you from the disabilities, dementia or other manifestations of your chronic illness is to use a revocable living trust. There is no more powerful mechanism to protect you through disability. This same technique, the living trust, can easily be used to avoid probate. In fact, this is the most common use of living trusts. Thus, planning to manage your assets during disability may also avoid probate. See Chapter 10.

ESTATE TAXES

For wealthy taxpayers seeking to minimize estate taxes, who also suffer from a chronic illness, the core of planning and the modifications are similar to those discussed in this book. So even wealthy readers can benefit from all the topics discussed in this book. However, those with large estates will have to layer this book's planning ideas with the tax, asset protection, and other planning typically pursued by wealthy taxpayers. Issues of competency, time frame, management, and so on need to be considered regardless of wealth. Therefore, details of actual tax strategies are beyond the scope of this book.

The federal estate tax does not apply in 2008 unless your estate (the net value of all you own) exceeds $2 million. This figure is scheduled to increase to $3.5 million in 2009. While it's impossible to determine what changes might occur with the federal estate tax, it's fairly safe to assume that you'd have to be in the wealthiest couple of percent of the country in terms of net worth to have to be concerned. If you have anywhere near that amount of money, you need to hire an estate planning attorney, and you can afford to do so. This book will still give you a lot of information to tailor your customized estate plan to address planning with a chronic illness, but you should not even consider using the sample forms. Too many estate planning and will books focus on taxes when it is simply not an issue for the vast majority of Americans. Try this statistic on for size. Only 18,431 estates filed estate tax returns with the IRS in 2004. That was less than 1 percent of the estates of all people who died in 2004 (.8 percent, to be exact).

The figure should be lower in later years as the amount you can give away at death without an estate tax increases. And hey, if you have that kind of money you certainly can afford an attorney to customize documents. So what is all the fuss about the evil death tax? Well, it might just have something to do with politics and not reality. But for the majority of people with a chronic disease, the estate tax is a distraction from the real planning issues. Not to say that tax planning isn't important; it is. Income tax issues are significant too. Assets owned on death get a "step up in basis." This means that the cost or investment in those assets is increased to the fair value at death, which can avoid all capital gains tax. Many states have estate or inheritance taxes that begin at much lower levels then the federal amount. But again, if taxes can be an issue, get professional help for all your planning. But whatever you do, don't lose your focus on taking care of yourself and addressing the nuances of your chronic illness in all your planning documents.

MEDICAID AND SIMILAR PLANNING

Medicaid is a government program that provides certain benefits to persons with minimal resources. There are many planning issues that those living with chronic illness need to address. In fact, from a financial perspective, qualifying for these programs may be the most important step you can take to secure your financial future. These matters, however, will not be addressed to a significant degree in this book, other than a brief discussion of how they impact provisions your family or loved ones may wish to include in their estate planning documents to protect you. See Chapter 12. Medicaid and similar planning has been addressed in other books and resources available to those living with chronic illness. To address it here would only detract from the focus of this book, and the information contained herein is not available elsewhere.

CHAPTER SUMMARY

This chapter has provided an introduction and overview to what the estate planning process is about, and how it must be modified to address the nuances of a range of different chronic illnesses. In order to protect yourself, estate and financial planning is vital. However, the planning that is "standard" and applicable for the "typical" person simply won't suffice to address your needs. The following chapters address each of the important issues and documents you'll need to address estate planning and your special needs.

CHAPTER 3

ORGANIZING LEGAL, FINANCIAL, AND OTHER INFORMATION
THE KEY TO YOUR SECURITY

WHY IT IS VITAL TO ORGANIZE YOUR INFORMATION

IF YOU DON'T KNOW WHAT YOU HAVE, you cannot plan for it. Pretty simple and straightforward. Everyone undertaking estate and financial planning needs to start by organizing all of their legal, financial, tax, and other important information. Organization is essential to your proper investment planning, assuring appropriate insurance coverage, optimal ownership (titling) of assets, and determining what type of estate planning documents you need. Organization of your records and documents is a prerequisite to your estate planning:

❖ Your will governs only those assets that pass through your estate (probate). If you have a brokerage account that is POD (pay on death) to a niece, it will pass automatically to her on your death. Your will is irrelevant. Accurate financial data is essential to determine how your assets will be distributed at death. Filling in a cheap will on an internet site won't provide you with this type of guidance.

❖ Making sure you have proper property and casualty insurance requires an understanding of what assets you have.

❖ A durable power of attorney, an essential document for everyone (especially someone with a chronic illness), is of limited practical use if your agent doesn't have the necessary information to act.

❖   A revocable living trust is the most powerful estate and financial planning tool to protect you. But to gain the optimal benefit of this tool, you and your advisers have to identify which assets can, and which cannot, be transferred to your living trust.

Because you have a chronic illness, this step takes on even greater importance. No matter what your prognosis, it is more likely that a time will come when you are unable to complete all necessary tasks yourself and will require the assistance of others. You want to be hyperorganized and keep all your records as simple as possible. The old KISS principal (keep it simple, stupid) should be your goal. If your disease may cause cognitive symptoms, you may one day reach a point where you will not be able to instruct people what to do and how to act or give them pertinent information. Organizing everything before that point will ensure an easier time for all concerned. Even if your disease has no cognitive symptoms, you may become bedridden, hospitalized, or may require surgery, during which you are unable to perform these tasks yourself. By systematically categorizing and labeling all important documents, you can make attending to your needs a simple task for your agent and your loved ones who help out.

❖   The more organized your documents and finances are, the easier it will be for you to retain as much control yourself, as long as possible. If you can consolidate all your financial assets into one institution, preferably with a single statement for all of your accounts, they will be easier to monitor, especially if you experience cognitive issues.

❖   If your affairs are clear, simple, and organized, you can remain involved and in control to the maximum extent possible, turning over the portions of your finances you need help with incrementally, rather than all at one time.

❖   Depending on how your illness progresses, you may eventually need someone to take over portions of the financial and administrative work. The easier, more organized, and more automatic, the better they will do. This will allow your agent to spend the most time working on what you need, not scrambling to find important documents.

❖   Organization will create an easily identifiable history of what you've done in the past. This can provide valuable guidance for those helping you out if at some future point you cannot communicate your wishes. For example, a computerized checkbook will point out your pattern of gifts, charitable donations, and so on.

How to Organize Your Information

A simple and effective way to organize your important documents and information is to set up a primary loose-leaf binder in which you will store most, if not all, of your documents. You may want to keep in mind that if you suffer from joint pain or stiffness or motor problems, opening loose-leaf binders may become difficult for you, and an alternate solution could be a system of coded file folders, perhaps in a rolling bin. The advantage of a binder over folders is that papers won't fall out and get lost. An in-between approach that is easier if you have hand dexterity issues but is less prone to papers falling out, is an accordion file sold in office supply stores. Figure out what works best for you, and if the approach you've chosen becomes impractical or difficult, you can always change.

Whatever filing system you use, the next step is to create tabs and label them for each of the categories of documents contained in your primary binder. Taking some time to plan out how you will organize your financial and legal documents is important. You want a simple approach that makes it readily obvious to anyone coming in to help you what is filed where. As your cognitive abilities decline, it will be easier to stay on top of everything. Color coding (e.g., tabs for legal documents in blue, assets in green, liabilities and credit cards in red, etc.) can help too. If you have a complex situation with respect to a particular tab/category, you need to set up a separate supplemental loose-leaf binder for those documents. Depending on your situation, you may need to use one or more supplementary loose-leaf binders in addition to your primary binder.

EXAMPLE

Let's assume you have a home-based business. In your primary binder, you might include summary data on the business and indicate that there is a separate binder or folder system for the business. This way, you can break out the business documents and finances with appropriate detail to be helpful to you or someone helping you out without cluttering your general finances and legal records.

These properly organized binders (folders or other files) are necessary to identify the planning steps that can improve your legal, tax, or financial situation. Any time you set up a supplementary binder to handle paperwork in a particular area, be sure to reference that supplemental binder in your primary binder. Thus any heir, agent, business partner, etc., will be directed to the additional information.

These are possible sections to consider when organizing your filing system. If one does not apply, you may omit it. Add additional components or sections that might make sense for you.

1.   Contents
2.   Emergency
3.   Basic background info
4.   Medical and health information
5.   Banking and financial info
6.   Credit cards and liabilities
7.   Securities and other investments
8.   Insurance info
9.   Estate planning documents
10.   Tax info
11.   Business interests
12.   Personal property
13.   Real estate records
14.   Retirement asset info
15.   Miscellaneous assets
16.   Wallet
17.   Budgeting

WHERE TO KEEP YOUR RECORDS, DOCUMENTS, AND INFORMATION

Once you have assembled and organized your documents into a binder or folder system, you need to decide where to place them so they can be easily reached in an emergency. If you have a filing cabinet or a home office, it may be a good idea to store your binder there, since it will probably be the first place someone will look. It is also important to inform your agents, spouse, and other loved ones about the location of your documents, so they have easy access to everything in case of an emergency. Keep in mind, that if your disease includes cognitive symptoms, this system may also be designed to assist you as your disease progresses. So keep your binder somewhere that is easily accessible and logical for you (i.e., in a place you usually keep things of this kind, not hidden in some location you seldom use or see). A fire-proof file cabinet might be an ideal location.

COMPUTERIZE YOUR FINANCES

One of the most productive things you can do is to computerize your finances and related matters. The cost of computers has declined dramatically over the years, while the capabilities have increased. The most significant benefit of computerization is that you can automate many tasks, which makes it safer and easier for you to keep in control of your affairs longer. Here are some of the ways computerization can help:

❖ If your checkbook and investment accounts are computerized, you can use a large screen to magnify text or have voice software to make it easier to deal with documents. This can be great if you have optic neuritis or other complications.

❖ You can easily back up to a CD or DVD to store off site or even use an online backup service that will automatically back up your data over the internet every night. The more you automate, the easier it is to manage.

❖ You can set up automatic monthly bill paying and reminders for other clerical tasks such as checking your free credit report from one of the three main credit agencies every four months, etc.

❖ Online bill payments can help you avoid many tasks that are or may become difficult as a result of dexterity or other issues. No more envelopes, stamps, etc. This means you can avoid the envelope stuffing and other tasks that may be difficult for you.

❖ You can easily back up selected data to give to your accountant to help you with tax planning or returns. If you want to save money and your returns are simple, it's easy to import your data from a computerized checkbook into a tax preparation program and do returns on your own. That not only can be a huge money saver, but it also eliminates additional efforts involved in dealing with an outside accountant. However, if your situation is complex or you have a business, spend the money and make the effort to use a qualified CPA.

❖   Budgeting is essential to investment and estate planning. (If you run out of money your will won't be of much use!) Most computerized checkbook and financial programs have simple, powerful, and easy to use budgeting functions. The reports that you can easily print and use will help you complete most of the important budgeting steps. In addition, if you maintain your personal checkbook and financial account records in such a program, a printout of your net worth statement (or perhaps a balance sheet if you operate a business) will be a helpful add-on to your documents. This report will also include much of the data your estate planner needs.

What Information to Organize

ESTATE PLANNING DOCUMENTS

Once you've finalized and signed all the appropriate documents discussed in this book, you need to organize them to make them accessible to those who will help you. You should sign only one original will. Depending on what your attorney advises, you might sign as many as three originals of each of the other documents. This will enable you to retain an original of each, with other signed originals going to your agent or other fiduciary (e.g., trustee) and your lawyer. Below is a breakdown of where documents can be kept. In all events, you should keep a copy behind a tab (or in a file) labeled something like "Estate Planning Documents." If your original is in your safe deposit box, safe, etc., you can note on your copy where the original is kept.

❖   **Power of attorney.** An original with your lawyer, an original with the first agent (person named in the power to help you with your financial and legal matters), a copy with each successor agent (the agents who serve if your first agent can't), an original with your personal papers. You might also give a copy to your financial planner (wealth manager).

❖   **Living will.** An original with your lawyer, an original with the first agent (person named in the power to help with your health care decisions if you cannot), a copy with each successor agent (the agents who serve if your first agent can't), an original with your personal papers. You might also give a copy to your attending physicians (e.g., your internist and neurologist).

❖ **HIPAA release.** An original with your lawyer, an original with the first agent (person named in the power to help with monitoring your medical issues), and an original with your personal papers. You might also give an original to your attending physician(s).

❖ **Health care proxy.** An original with your lawyer, an original with the first agent (person named in the power to help with your health care decisions if you cannot), a copy with each successor agent (the agents who serve if your first agent can't), and an original with your lawyer. You might also give a copy to each attending physician and specifically request that it be added to your medical records. This should basically be the same as your living will.

❖ **Will.** In most cases, your lawyer should hold your original will. However, make sure that there will be no charge for your family to get the will if they opt to use another attorney after your death. You should also specifically inquire as to what steps your lawyer will take to safeguard your original will. Does the attorney hold it in a fireproof box (e.g., fire-rated safe or bank safe deposit box)? How does the attorney track original wills? If the attorney is a sole practitioner, what happens if he or she dies? You should have a copy. Whether you give your executor (and successor executor) a copy depends on the circumstances. You may not want to distribute copies of your will in case your feelings change and you want to change who inherits your assets.

❖ **Living trust.** If you sign only one original living trust, you might want your lawyer to hold it in safekeeping along with your will. Alternatively, you might keep the original and give photocopies to your lawyer and cotrustee. It's also advisable to give copies to your successor trustees as they will be responsible for your protection and for managing your finances if your health deteriorates to the point you cannot serve or if the other current trustees cannot serve. If they have a copy of the trust document in advance and are aware of their responsibilities, the transition from the current to the successor trustees will be smoother. Your accountant may want a copy of the trust for the permanent files that accountants typically maintain for clients. Finally, your bank and investment manager may want copies to open up trust bank and brokerage accounts.

OTHER LEGAL RECORDS

There are a number of other important legal documents for which you may want to organize tabs in your filing system. The following is a listing of some of the most common, with a brief explanation of how and why you might need them for your estate planning.

❖   **Deed.** Your home may be your largest asset, so the legal document that confirms your ownership is important. You might keep a copy of the deed behind the tab (or in a file) labeled "House." You might also keep a copy of the title insurance policy (insurance of your ownership of the house) and other important records in the same location. The deed is vital for your estate planner as verification of how your house is owned (titled). It is essential to your plan that the ownership of your home be consistent with your other planning.

❖   **Divorce agreement.** If you're divorced, a copy of the agreement, and any ancillary documents (e.g., you might have a settlement agreement, a court decree, etc.) should be kept together. These documents are essential for your financial and estate planning as they may indicate important cash flow (e.g., alimony, child support) obligations you may have. There may also be important information related to assets shared with your ex-spouse. For example, your ex-husband might own half of your house, or you may own half of the house your ex-wife resides in. These facts are essential for your planners to know. Furthermore, after assembling all the relevant documents, you may want to make some notations as to how you've dealt with issues or responsibilities of the divorce; these can be invaluable to an agent or other fiduciary trying to help you.

❖   **Business documents.** The documents filed to set up your business.

FINANCIAL RECORDS

❖   **Life insurance policies.** If you own any insurance, you'll likely want to keep it in force, especially if you purchased it before you were diagnosed with your illness. Details on the policy are vital for a host of reasons. The policy should be periodically reviewed to make certain that it is performing as anticipated, and to determine if there are any options under the policy you should take advantage of. For example, let's say you purchased a term policy prior to your diagnosis, if the policy has a conversion option permitting you to convert the policy to a permanent policy that will never lapse, that is an economically prudent opportunity that should be addressed. If you have difficulty paying increased premiums, you might be able to borrow funds or sell a portion or all of the policy. Your estate planner will need your insurance information to review whether you should establish a trust to own the policy (not the revocable living trust discussed in this book, but rather an irrevocable life insurance trust), etc.

❖ **Brokerage statements, bank statements, etc.** You need the data on your various accounts to assemble the balance sheet your lawyer and other planners need. The manner in which those accounts are owned (titled) is also vital to share with these individuals. If the account is joint, the joint owner might automatically obtain ownership of the account on your death. If the account has a beneficiary designation, your planners need to have a copy, as your designation may determine who will inherit the account.

❖ **Retirement accounts.** Copies of account statements, beneficiary designations, plan summary documents (if available), etc., should be filed behind a tab labeled "Retirement Plans."

❖ **Disability insurance coverage.**

PERSONAL AND FAMILY RECORDS

The following family records are important to assemble:

❖ Listing of key family members, including parents, siblings, spouse, children, and grandchildren. Provide address, age, and other relevant data for each person listed, and note whether anyone on your list is deceased or divorced. Note any additional information you consider significant.

❖ Birth certificate.

❖ Marriage certificate.

❖ Other key documents.

MEDICAL RECORDS

You should include key medical data in your primary binder and then set up a separate binder that has all pertinent information concerning your health care, particularly with respect to your illness and the unique issues you have to cope with:

❖   Medical and health insurance

❖   Long-term care insurance

❖   General medical information

❖   Nutrition, diet, and related information

❖   Medication

❖   Psychological information

❖   Neurologist

❖   Internist

❖   MRIs

❖   Lab reports

❖   Travel data and resources

EMERGENCY INFORMATION

A listing of important names, phone numbers, account numbers, and other data that you or someone helping you can quickly find. This should be the first file or tab in your primary binder.

PROFESSIONALS YOU MAY USE TO ORGANIZE AND PLAN

To have these issues addressed properly, you need an attorney who devotes a substantial part of his practice to nothing but estate planning. You may also want to hire a financial planner, in addition to any accountants or insurance agents you already retain. Your planning will benefit greatly from consulting with all of these professionals, and you may want to meet with all of them at the same time, thus allowing them (and you) to discuss your estate plan together. Utilizing all of your professionals to the best of their abilities will greatly benefit your estate.

SAMPLE FORMS TO ORGANIZE YOUR RECORDS

Scores of free forms to use in organizing your various financial, legal, and other records can be obtained from www.laweasy.com.

CHAPTER SUMMARY

This chapter has provided guidance and suggestions for organizing your financial, estate, legal, and other documents. Once these documents are organized, copies of certain documents need to be disseminated to the people you will be relying on. Finally, you need to use the information you have assembled as part of your estate planning process.

CHAPTER 4

COMPETENCY
TAKING LEGAL ACTIONS TO PROTECT YOURSELF

WHAT IS COMPETENCY?

COMPETENCY IS A LEGAL CONCEPT, not a psychological one. In terms of estate planning, it is about convincing a judge or jury that a document in question (e.g., a will, trust, power of attorney) is a fair expression of a reasonably healthy judgment. The esoteric psychological constructs are not really helpful. They are only constructs or labels that might be used to facilitate what one would consider a just conclusion under given circumstances. The attorney must prove that you should or should not be declared competent. That is not a scientific determination; it is getting someone to believe that a person ought to be declared competent or not. Look at it in human terms of what you were hoping to accomplish. If "ordinary folk" would find it unusual, it is a problem. If it's what many people might do, then it is likely to be accepted.

Many people mistakenly believe competency is purely a medical concept, when in fact competency is really a legal determination. Your lawyer, not only your physician, will have to be involved in the process of determining whether you are legally competent. People assume a single or uniform definition exists for competency. In fact, there are a host of differences, and the law recognizes various incarnations of the term. The degree of competency to sign a will (testamentary capacity) is less than that required to execute a contract (contractual capacity). The circumstances of the specific matter weigh on how competency in that situation should be assessed. Assessing competency is a function of what degree of capacity a specific legal action requires. The more complex the matter, the greater the degree of competency required.

Timing is critical. The question in many competency challenges is not "whether" you were incompetent, but "when" you became incompetent. With Alzheimer's disease, dementia will occur. Therefore, the tough issue is to determine when the degree of dementia is too great for you to take estate planning steps. At what point in time will you no longer have the competency to sign estate planning contracts (e.g., a contract to sell an interest in a family business to a child or family trust), or to sign a valid will, or take other similar steps.

Establishing with some specificity at what point in the time continuum your competency waned or when you lapsed into incompetence is often problematic and can often be center of a legal challenge. If you signed an estate planning document while deemed competent, the contractual arrangement should be respected. If you were not capable of understanding the transaction, the IRS or an heir may overturn the arrangement. For example, if you wanted to favor your son who took regular care of you during your illness and provide a lesser bequest to your daughter who was seemingly indifferent to your health struggles, the issue of your competency to do so could be critical. (See Chapter 12.)

Determining your level of capacity is vital in order to ascertain what actions may be appropriately taken. If your attorney has more than a mild question as to your competency, he or she will likely evaluate the need for you to have a formal competency assessment. This could entail having your attending physician provide an evaluation of your physical condition with an emphasis on how it may impact your competency, your neurologist or psychiatrist providing an evaluation of your mental capacity, and your attorney making a final conclusion as to competency.

TESTAMENTARY CAPACITY

Testamentary capacity refers to whether you have the competence to sign a will. This requires that you know the natural objects of your bounty (children, grandchildren, etc.), understand the nature and extent of your property (what assets you own, your balance sheet), and the relationship of both to make a rational distribution in your will. Some definitions require that you have sufficient mind and memory and be capable of understanding the general nature of the matter in which you are engaged, namely, making a will. You should also understand the interrelationship of these factors. Capacity is required only when your will is executed, so that the will is executed during a lucid interval, and your attorney must be able to demonstrate that this in fact occurred. You can be incapacitated before and after the execution with no legal consequences. The level of capacity that you must have to execute a will is relatively low and less than the requisite capacity to execute the contractual documents often included in an estate and financial plan. A person may, in fact, execute a will even if classified by her physician as insane, feeble-minded, a drug addict, and even suffering at times from a partial loss of memory related to person and things.

CONTRACTUAL CAPACITY

This refers to the competency you must have to sign a contract. For you to have contractual capacity, you must generally understand the nature and effect of the act and the business being transacted. If the business being transacted is highly complicated, a higher level of understanding may be needed. Having sufficient capacity to execute a will does not demonstrate your capacity to sign or enter into a contract, because a greater degree of capacity is necessary to understand this more complex transaction. For many business documents (e.g., partnership agreement), the document itself may include its own definition for disability, including issues of competency. In such instances, you or your attorney needs to review the governing legal document. The threshold level of competency for you to retain shares and a directorship in a closely held business may be much more stringent than the level of competency that is required to contract in general.

POWER OF ATTORNEY

A power of attorney is a document in which you designate a person (agent) to handle your financial affairs if you can't. (See Chapter 5.) The capacity required to execute a power of attorney varies by jurisdiction. In some states, only capacity similar to that required to sign a will (testamentary capacity) is required. In others, the capacity to contract is required.

LIVING WILL AND HEALTH PROXY

These are documents used to address your health care decisions. (See Chapter 7.) Capacity to execute these documents is tied to the legal doctrine of informed consent. A patient has the right to control contact with his or her person. Informed consent to such contact requires that the patient provide voluntary, competent, and informed consent. Although some courts have held that the capacity to provide informed consent is similar to the capacity required to contract, the law in this regard is not clear and clinical models of capacity are therefore often used instead.

WHY COMPETENCY MATTERS

Determining competency is a critical issue for many estate plans, as well as many tax audits. Competency is the prerequisite to the validity of any estate plan, but remains widely misunderstood. If you are not competent, then any document you sign or any transaction you complete, will be ineffectual. That's significant. Unfortunately, what constitutes competency is an issue often misunderstood. The trend of our aging population raises more and more questions about issues of competency, and these issues will be raised with more frequency over time. Furthermore, the ever-growing pharmacopoeia of treatments for diseases that afflict the elderly resulting in lengthened lifespan will bring even more complexity to the competency analysis.

CHRONIC ILLNESS AND COMPETENCY MISCONCEPTIONS

There are many misconceptions about competency, especially with respect to people with chronic illness. Many people, for example, assume that everyone with a chronic illness is incompetent. Many people also incorrectly assume that a Parkinsonian masked face implies incompetence. While some chronic illnesses do result in dementia, like Alzheimer's disease, many, such as multiple sclerosis, may not. Although some people living with MS will suffer cognitive impact, in the vast majority of cases MS does not result in the type of incompetence that can prevent people from managing their affairs or making important decisions. And while it is true that people with MS may need assistance with their financial and legal affairs during an attack (exacerbation), it is also true that many can resume control over such affairs once the attack has passed. This on-again/off-again condition is confusing and misunderstood by probably almost anyone not familiar with MS and its symptoms. The nuances of how each chronic illness impacts competency can be quite delicate and differ from one illness to the next, even among different people living with the same chronic illness. Generalizations are dangerous, and the burden will be on you to reprove those that are incorrect.

CHRONIC ILLNESS, COMPETENCY, AND DANGEROUS ASSUMPTIONS

Many people, including professional advisers, erroneously assume that those living with many types of chronic illnesses must have significant cognitive impairment. It's easy to make such generalizations, but inaccurate generalizations can be damaging to your interactions with your estate planning professionals and your ability to obtain the proper advice. If your will is challenged, a jury might well have the same misconceptions about your cognition. It is therefore important that your estate planner and other professionals are adequately versed on what constitutes mental incapacity and what does not, especially in the case of chronic illness where it is likely to be an issue. They must, above all, recognize that chronic illnesses, as well as their impact on those who live with them, are not identical.

KEY

> **You must communicate in clear detail to all your advisers what your current cognitive situation is, what it will likely become, and over what approximate time period.**

OVERVIEW OF CHRONIC ILLNESSES AND COGNITIVE ISSUES: FACTS AND FIGURES

DEMENTIA AND COMPETENCY

Dementia is deterioration in cognitive function, often as part of a progressive illness that reaches a level or degree that impacts your daily life. It is usually defined in terms of a decline in memory accompanied by other cognitive impairments. There are a number of causes of dementia, but Alzheimer's disease (AD) accounts for approximately 70 percent of dementias in Americans age 71 or older. Vascular dementia, which is caused by a decrease in blood flow to the brain typically as a result of a stroke, accounts for about 17 percent of all dementias. Other causes such as mixed dementia, dementia with Lewy bodies, and Parkinson's disease account for the remaining 13 percent of dementias. Cognitive decline has a host of implications to the estate planning process:

- ❖　It creates a sense of urgency to complete planning while feasible.

- ❖　It determines and corroborates whether you are competent to complete a particular plan, or to sign a particular document.

- ❖　It signals the need for planning for potentially long-term disability.

MULTIPLE SCLEROSIS AND COMPETENCY

Cognitive impairment affects many of those living with MS. There is not necessarily a correlation between visible physical impairment and cognitive impairment. MS is quite enigmatic in that conclusions can't be drawn from your physical condition about the likelihood of current or future cognitive impairment. A significant number of those with MS may have some cognitive impairment, but most will not. Your cognitive impairment, if any, may affect certain activities but not the ability to make many of the executive decisions often assumed an issue for those who are "disabled." Given this uncertainty, the focus of planning should be to provide you with maximum control over your financial and legal matters, while creating an appropriate safety net in the event cognitive impairment becomes sufficiently significant as to require it. Even when assistance is required, the best approach is one that allows you to remain involved, as a cofiduciary (e.g., a cotrustee of a revocable living trust), an approach in which the burden can be shared but does not eliminate your involvement in your financial and legal affairs.

PARKINSON'S DISEASE AND COMPETENCY

As many as one-half of people with PD have difficulties with memory and thought processing. These difficulties, however, are not simple to evaluate or always obvious. For example, even if you have a cognitive impact from your PD, the implications of that impact can vary from inconsequential to substantial depending on the demands placed on you. A misconception is that many laypeople use an Alzheimer's paradigm for understanding PD cognitive impact, even though the cognitive impact of Alzheimer's is often not relevant to someone with PD. Someone with PD may be able to function normally while having some issues with disorganization, distractibility, prioritizing, and forgetfulness.

Depression and apathy affect many people with PD, sometimes making them reluctant to schedule a meeting or follow up on the recommendations from professional advisers. In such cases, the encouragement and involvement of other family members may be critical to the planning process. It is helpful, in this situation, to inform your advisers that they should not misinterpret apathy towards planning as a sign that they should not continue to push the process forward. Consideration should also be given to authorizing communications between your attorney, your agents and family members, and your other advisers. This can prevent questions about ethical issues and facilitates coordination and communication among those who may need to work together on your behalf.

All of these are appropriate and vital steps that can protect you before cognitive deterioration reaches a level where options begin to be foreclosed. These steps should be addressed in a manner that preserves your independence if deterioration occurs and especially in the event it never occurs. Your planning must be flexible enough for you to maintain control over your life and retain dignity, regardless of the course your PD takes.

If you have PD, addressing the possibility of cognitive issues should be considered in tandem with an understanding that PD is often accompanied by other health issues, especially for people of advanced age. These other health issues may increase the likelihood of cognitive impairment and dramatically change the planning that is appropriate, or the urgency in completing your planning. It is therefore important to inform your attorney about your overall health status and about which other conditions, if any, may have an impact on you.

ALZHEIMER'S AND COMPETENCY

If you have Alzheimer's disease, your estate planning documents should reflect the likelihood that arrangements made and documents executed today are likely to be permanent rather than subject to modification. With a definite trajectory of cognitive decline, you may not have the luxury of revisiting and revising plans and documents and must plan for what will likely be years of disability during which other people will have to handle your financial, legal, and other matters. The biggest challenge may be completing these arrangements as you approach the fringe of competency.

You will most likely require the help of family members, friends, and others to get through the emotional difficulties of making tough decisions, which most people engaging in estate planning consider theoretical.

AD symptoms are often divided into stages (mild, moderate, severe, and profound). Even at the "mild" stage of AD, you may become disoriented as to time, date, or place. This may make attending to planning and document execution somewhat difficult. To prevent or withstand a future challenge for competency or undue influence, however, you must be able to demonstrate that at the time of execution you had sufficient understanding of the issues involved and the import of what was being done.

Even at the mild stage of AD, you may have difficulty with math calculations and may find it difficult to balance a checkbook. The loss of executive function (organizational and complex decision-making skills) can occur even in the mild form of AD. While you might readily have the level of capacity to sign a will, if you struggle to balance a checkbook, you may not have sufficient competency to understand sophisticated estate planning mechanisms like charitable lead trusts (CLTs), grantor retained annuity trusts (GRATs), and so on. If you do not, there is a risk that the efficacy of these estate mechanisms may be undermined by a competency challenge.

WHAT YOUR ESTATE PLANNER SHOULD KNOW AND DO

There are a number of points your estate planner should consider in helping you. You might want to discuss this list with your planner:

❖   Don't make assumptions.

❖   Understand that there is tremendous variability among those living with chronic illness. There is even significant variability between those with the same illness. Even more confusing, there can be significant variability in the symptoms experienced at different times by the same client, even during the same meeting.

❖   Whatever the negative cognitive impact you have because of your chronic illness, it is likely to worsen absent a breakthrough in research. Therefore, planning should not be deferred for long.

❖   When implementing estate and tax planning, consideration should be given to corroborating your competency to avoid challenges at a later date. This should be done even if you have no significant cognitive impairment, given the ignorance of so many people about the effects of chronic illness.

❖ You may have the mental capacity to sign a will (called "testamentary capacity"), but may not have the capacity to engage in more complex contractual transactions, such as a sale of a family business interest to a defective grantor dynasty trust.

❖ Your assets should be consolidated and simplified. It is easier when living with a chronic illness, especially one with worsening cognitive issues, to interact with a single integrated wealth manager than with a half-dozen or more banks, brokerage firms, and other investment professionals.

❖ Follow meetings and substantive phone conversations with an action list of prioritized bullet points that you must address. This should not be a multiple page memo, but a concise and clear bullet list of items.

❖ Break the planning process into distinct phases, each to be accomplished sequentially to facilitate completing the process in a manner that is easier for you. For example, Phase I might be to complete powers of attorney, living wills, HIPAA releases, and health proxies. Phase II might be to complete a revocable living trust and will. Phase III might address beneficiary designations, insurance, and an insurance trust. More sophisticated planning might be handled as Phase IV. Discrete, logically organized, and sequential steps will be much easier.

❖ Observe your conduct for signs of diminished capacity, paying attention to factors that suggest change. These might include comments from a spouse or family member. You might (and should) raise the issue yourself if you can.

❖ Consider whether a Folstein Mini-Mental State Exam may be administered as a means of documenting your status. This entails responding to a series of questions and performing certain actions, all of which are scored. The range of scores provides an indication normal, borderline, or impaired capacity. There are a host of other screening methodologies that can be used.

❖ Assess the degree of physical, financial, or other harm to you from the transaction involved. For example, giving a caregiver a power of attorney to control your financial assets is far riskier than signing a will that divides an estate equally between your natural children.

❖ Analyze your ability to articulate the reasoning leading to a decision, your ability to understand the consequences of that decision, and whether the decision is consistent with your long-term goals and values. Retention of prior meeting notes to demonstrate a consistent pattern of thought and planning may support your ability to make a particular testamentary disposition.

❖ Weigh what documents are being signed, the complexity of the documents overall (the big picture), and any other relevant circumstances.

❖ Document observations of your capacity as well as observations of other professionals involved. For example, two lawyers in the firm each meet separately with you for interviews and each independently documents discussions and observations.

❖ If you have an illness, like Alzheimer's, that is likely to progress to the point where a guardian or conservator may be necessary, your attorney should advise you to designate the person and successors that you would want to serve as guardian while you are competent to do so. Many states will permit this.

❖ If your capacity has diminished to the point where new documents cannot be signed, then efforts should be directed to reviewing and implementing existing documents and planning, regardless of their shortcomings. Often planning goals can be achieved even with inadequate existing documents through creative use of title to assets, interpretations or permitted modifications of existing documents, or court intervention.

❖ Your attorney should question whether your actions are rational, expected, and appropriate. For example, have you selected an appropriate beneficiary (one or more of your children) or made a choice that might be considered aberrational (e.g., leaving everything to your health aide)? It is much easier to prove that "normal" behavior is acting in a manner that benefits your children rather then a home health aide. If your attorney must one day address your decision when establishing your competency, the latter choice might be evidence that you did something contrary to what normal expectation would be and raise questions about other decisions you made while ill.

❖ Obtain appropriate physician letters, attesting to your physical and mental status and indicating any medical issues that may have an impact on your cognitive functions. For example, it may be helpful to have a letter from an internist stating that there are no medical issues that might impair your cognitive capacity. However, this letter must be precise to be of any value. If vague terms like "normal" or phrases like "patient has excellent judgment" are used, what do they mean? Without clear and defined terms, a letter from an attending physician may have little relevance. The physician letter should provide details of the examination given, your current medical condition, the results of a current physical examination, whether there are medical issues that require further inquiry (e.g., unexplained symptoms or symptoms that might be explained by a serious disability that may affect cognition), a psycho-social history, a description of your current living circumstances, etc. The physician letter should also confirm that you were questioned about people, places, and time. The questions and your responses should be documented.

❖ Make documents understandable. This is quite a challenge when dealing with tax complexities and other complicated matters. No court or jury will believe that you understood a document if they cannot understand it. If a jury cannot understand what your will or other documents intend, they are likely to suspect your competency to sign it. Documents must be sufficiently clear, with consideration to the unavoidable complexity of tax and other laws, so that the average person can understand them. Anything that makes a document intelligible to a layperson is helpful. Often all this requires is a simple, explanatory, and lead-in sentence. When the complexity necessitated by tax laws, property laws (e.g., rule against perpetuities), asset protection, and other steps makes a simple document an impossibility, your attorney should make it easier to comprehend with captions or other devices that make the information simpler.

❖ "To videotape or not to videotape." If William Shakespeare, Esq., had been an estate planner, that would have been the question. If your lawyer records you signing a will, certain conditions must be observed. First, you must state your intention regarding the distribution of property and that it is your wish that the will not be challenged. This should be done as you look right into the camera as talking directly to the judge or jury. If, however, you know that the video will not support your competency (e.g., because of Parkinson masked face, tremors from another chronic illness, etc.) your attorney should not attempt to video tape your will signing.

❖ If a clinical evaluation must be made as to your competency, your attorney should select the appropriate clinician to undertake the analysis. In many cases, this would be a mental health professional who is knowledgeable about the specific health problems you face (e.g., a neurologist with expertise in Alzheimer's), familiar with the various assessment approaches relevant to the issue of determining capacity in relation to your illness, and has considerable experience conducting competency evaluations.

❖　　Your attorney should then take appropriate actions in response to the above findings and determine what steps should be taken to protect you. For example, if you are competent but have a progressive or chronic illness that will lessen capacity over time, your attorney should update all documents and planning, review in detail a durable power of attorney, and other steps.

EXAMPLE • *Alzheimer's Disease*

Jim Powell is 81 and has been diagnosed with Alzheimer's. AD results in dementia and is fatal. There are two characteristics of AD, tangles and plaques. A protein called "tau" accumulates in abnormal deposits in neuron pathways in the brain called "microtubules." Normally, nutrients are transported to brain cells and waste away from the brain through microtubules. Eventually, microtubules collapse into what is referred to as "tangles." Plaques are microscopic accumulations of beta-amyloid fragments. As the tangles and plaques expand, Jim's memory and other functions decline. Nerve cells lose their ability to communicate and AD progresses. As this spreads, brain tissues die, and impairment accelerates. Jim's estate planning attorney and financial planner meet to review a revised estate plan and investment allocation. The attorney becomes concerned about Jim's capacity, especially in light of the diagnosis of Alzheimer's, and contacts Jim's attending neurologist. After obtaining the appropriate HIPAA release (see below), the attorney requests an evaluation report that addresses a number of issues, including the medical diagnosis, its impact on capacity, and Jim's location on the disease time continuum and his likely progression. The report should also include evidence of cognitive issues regarding Jim's understanding or processing of information, memory loss, evidence of behavioral issues, other health issues that may aggravate Alzheimer's (e.g., mixed dementia, which can include elements of both Alzheimer's and vascular dementia), as well as the medications Jim is taking, when they were started, and their impact on Jim's life, activities, and ability to understand legal documents and transactions. The attorney also requests that the report detail Jim's history, including personal, physical, psychological and situational conditions as his values and preferences are relevant to his health care decisions, long-term care coverage, and disposition of his assets. This cognitive and behavioral assessment is the basis on which Jim's attorney will determine Jim's legal capacity for executing the revised estate planning and investment allocation documents.

ADDITIONAL POINTS TO CONSIDER

❖   Your family or loved ones will need a formal signed HIPAA (Health Insurance Portability and Accountability Act of 1996) release to obtain medical records. It may, in fact, be advisable to obtain the release and medical records early in the process. Not only will this support the planning process, but it can be significantly easier to do so while you are functioning at your best, rather than at a later date when you may no longer be competent to sign the release.

❖   Your attorney should consider constructing a time line of events, including ancillary or tangential matters. Often a time line can truly tell a story demonstrating competency. The major points on the time line would be psychological examinations finding competency, physician letters attesting to competency or the lack of known physical conditions likely to negatively impact cognition, execution of a will or other legal documents where counsel and witnesses can attest to competency, etc. However, anecdotal evidence can also help tell the story you need.

EXAMPLE

If you are admitted to the hospital and discharged, what do the examinations prior to discharge indicate? Were the predischarge examinations really relevant to competency? Even an examination by a neurologist may be of little or modest benefit depending on the purpose and nature of the examination. Often a discharge summary may exist in the patient record. They may include innocuous comments such as "AOx3" (alert and oriented in all three spheres), a potentially positive and telling sign. But look beyond these significant events at other matters as well. What, for example, did the nursing notes say? Often these notes will describe a patient's conduct and behavior, something that may support competency or underscore cognitive impairment.

CHAPTER SUMMARY

Competency is the threshold issue to address in all planning. Because the degree of cognitive impact of various illnesses is so different and can change over time, this must be addressed for everyone living with chronic illness at some point and to some degree.

CHAPTER 5

Power of Attorney
Authorizing Someone to Take Legal Action for You

Introduction

IF YOU ARE SICK OR DISABLED, who can handle financial, legal, and tax matters for you? Who can pay your bills so your bank doesn't foreclose on your mortgage, or the utility company doesn't cut off your phone, electric, heat, and power? And who will take care of other emergencies that you are not able to handle?

If you are married, you cannot automatically count on your spouse to handle every emergency just because of the marital relationship. Don't assume that your spouse has legal authority to sign your name. He or she does not. If you have a joint checking account, your spouse can sign checks from that account because it is joint, not by virtue of being your spouse. That's not much to rely upon in an emergency.

The best answer to the questions posed above is a legal answer: power of attorney. A power of attorney is the most important and also the simplest estate planning document. It is a contract in which you (called the "grantor") delegate ("grant") to another person (called your "attorney in fact" or "agent") the power and right to act on your behalf in the event you are ill, injured, unavailable, or unable to act on your own behalf for any reason. Your agent is given the important responsibility of handling your financial matters in the event of any emergency, which prevents you from taking the necessary actions.

The power of attorney is one of the most important documents to consider during estate planning. But it is also one of the most frequently overlooked, and one of the most misunderstood. The power of attorney can be a very simple document, perhaps a one-page form purchased at a local stationery store. (But see discussion below on the risk of using this kind of form). A power of attorney can also be a far more complex and lengthy document prepared by an attorney to deal with a specific business transaction.

Important rules concerning power of attorney documents differ from state to state (e.g., what formalities are required to sign the power). Be certain to consult with an attorney in your state as to the specific rules that apply to you. For example, some states limit to certain close relatives the people you may name to act for you. In some states it may be advisable to file (record) your power of attorney in the appropriate governmental office, such as a county clerk. That will make it a public document so that anyone who has to rely upon it can find it in the public records.

While it is important that everyone over age 18 have a power of attorney, appointing an agent after being diagnosed with a chronic illness is even more important. Depending on your prognosis, you are likely to have a substantially greater need than the average person of your age to have someone step in to help you. Depending on your illness, this may even be a certainty. As with all of your estate planning documents, the impact of your diagnosis should result in modifications to the typical form, and you should consider adding detailed instructions to your agent. Will you suffer any cognitive impairment from your disease? How should that be addressed? The possible courses of your disease (not just the anticipated course) may lead you to consider the limits or allowances on the powers you give your agent under your power of attorney.

TERMINOLOGY USED IN POWERS OF ATTORNEY

Lawyers, like all specialists, love jargon. It's not that they're conspiring to make matters complicated—it's because the use of specific technical terms permits precision. Understanding some of the jargon used for powers of attorney will make it easier to work with your lawyer and plan and create the document you need.

POWER OF ATTORNEY

"Power of attorney" refers to the document in which you name a trusted person to be your agent and carry out your wishes.

DURABLE POWER OF ATTORNEY

The document is called a "durable" power of attorney because it gives your agent the right to act even in the event of your disability. If your power of attorney is not durable, it would become invalid upon your becoming disabled. That's not of much use, so the document should include a statement to the effect that: "This power of attorney will remain in force and effect even if I'm disabled." In most states, this is all that's necessary to achieve this important goal, however, requirements of applicable state law should be complied with in all cases. Check with a local attorney.

GENERAL POWER OF ATTORNEY

A general power enables your agent to take care of any matter that the power of attorney form or state law permits. This usually includes a very long and broad list of legal, financial, and other matters. In most, but not all situations, you would want a general power of attorney. The sample form illustrated in the appendix to this chapter is a general power of attorney. There are, however, some situations in which such a broad grant of power is not appropriate.

SPECIAL POWER OF ATTORNEY

A special power is a power that is limited in scope. It allows your agent to handle only one particular transaction or perhaps one type of transaction. A special power is useless for general planning if you become disabled because you don't know what legal and financial issues you're going to face and what problems will arise. Because you cannot possibly know what type of limited powers should be given to an agent under a special power of attorney, your best option for general protection and estate planning is to give someone a general power that will be broadly effective if you're disabled and that will enable your agent to handle any foreseeable financial matters. So why would you ever want a special or limited power? The examples below provide typical scenarios in which this type of power might apply.

EXAMPLE

Assume you're going out of town for a business meeting that cannot be canceled. Unfortunately, your contract for selling your house is scheduled to close that same week, and you have to be present at the closing to sign papers. What do you do? A special power of attorney could be an option. You could name a trusted friend or family member as your agent to sign any documents necessary to complete your house closing. This is a special power because you've only given the agent one limited right. After the house closing is completed, the agent's authority ends.

EXAMPLE

Assume you're selling your business because symptoms related to your illness have worsened. While you do pretty well on most days, some days are very tough. Not knowing how you will feel on the day of the closing, since the date has to be agreed upon well in advance, you have your lawyer who is handling the closing prepare a special durable power of attorney authorizing your agent to sign all the documents relating to the sale of the business "just in case." This is a special power because you've only given the agent one limited right, which is limited even further because the agent is authorized to act on your behalf only if you are too ill to do so yourself. After the sale of your business is completed, the agent's authority ends.

KEY

This is yet another example of why it is so important to ensure that your attorney and other advisors understand your illness and how it impacts you.

BUSINESS POWER

If you own or operate a business and are temporarily hospitalized or become incapacitated, who will sign checks, and address business or professional practice matters? Who will sign the payroll and other checks and ensure that your employees continue running the business if you are out? Improper planning can cause undue delay and hardship during an already difficult time, and this could be a significant problem. Properly prepared durable powers of attorney are an important part of the solution if your business or practice is organized as a "sole proprietorship." A sole proprietorship is simply a business you run personally, in contrast to a business that is organized in another form (corporation, limited liability company, partnership, etc.). A "special" power granted to a business adviser or colleague (or in the case of a professional practice, a similarly licensed professional) can be an essential aspect of protection.

Under certain circumstances, you may need to combine several documents. For example, you may wish to grant a limited power of attorney to a close colleague to authorize him or her to perform certain functions relating to your medical practice during a period when you are ill or otherwise unavailable. Such a power of attorney may even provide for compensation. You may execute another power of attorney granting your spouse the right to handle all personal financial matters. If your business is organized as a corporation, you may need to sign minutes or a unanimous written consent for the corporation naming the intended person as an officer of the corporation (e.g., vice president) in order to vest in this individual the powers needed to act on behalf of the corporation. The right approach is to consult your business attorney (often called "corporate" attorney) and make sure that you have appropriate precautions in place.

SPRINGING POWER OF ATTORNEY

Chronic illness creates a number of circumstances in which a springing power of attorney might be applicable. This power is one that only springs into use (i.e., your agent's power becomes effective) when you become disabled. This prevents your agent from having any authority until you are actually disabled and need assistance. This may be the best approach if you prefer not to grant any authority to your agent until it becomes absolutely necessary. The strongest argument against the springing power of attorney is that you should not grant any power of attorney unless you trust the person named. If trust is not an issue, why risk restricting the power of attorney until you become disabled? This could raise questions as to whether or when the power of attorney has become effective (i.e., whether you are disabled and when you actually became disabled). You could have a primary (first named) agent's power effective immediately upon signing your power of attorney (e.g., your spouse or partner), while the authority of alternate agents (children, friends) becomes effective only when those agents can legally demonstrate your disability. Some states do not recognize springing powers of attorney. If you feel comfortable naming certain people as agent if their power is effective only if you are disabled, consult an estate planning attorney in your state.

The typical advice for someone with a chronic illness is not to use a springing power of attorney, but rather to sign a power that is effective immediately. The rationale here is that you may be putting your agent (as well as yourself) in a precarious position because you are implicitly burdening that agent with the very real possibility that he or she will have to prove that you are disabled.

The problems of triggering a springing power are common to all people, not just those with chronic illness, but there are situations where it might be warranted and workable. Depending on the nature of your illness, the power may only have to be triggered once, when your level of incapacity reaches a point where an agent has to permanently take over. So if you have Alzheimer's disease, a springing power of attorney may not be unreasonable in that it will likely only have to be "sprung" once. Although your attorney may still maintain that a power of attorney that is effective upon signing is preferable, if you feel strongly about deferring the time until someone can act on your behalf, you can use a springing power of attorney.

More significantly, if your chronic illness is punctuated by flare-ups between which you can remain in control of your affairs, but during which you might need help, this generic advice is not particularly useful.

KEY

> You don't need to hire a specialist in estate planning for chronic illness or a financial planner that focuses on clients with chronic illness. Too often such advertised "specialties" are just a marketing gimmick. You want to hire competent professionals whom you can apprise in detail of your situation. A good estate planning attorney will quickly understand the nuances this book raises and will help tailor them to you to the extent deemed appropriate in his or her professional judgment.

IS YOUR CHRONIC ILLNESS PUNCTUATED BY SPORADIC FLARE-UPS?

Your chronic illness may follow an on-again, off-again pattern (i.e., intermittent flare-ups that are associated with relapsing-remitting MS, epilepsy, Crohn's disease, ulcerative colitis, rheumatoid arthritis, lupus, and other chronic illnesses). What this means is that you experience periods of relapse (when your symptoms increase in severity) and periods of remission (when you are relatively asymptomatic), and this may call for special planning alternatives.

Crohn's disease and ulcerative colitis are chronic digestive disorders of the intestines for which there are no cures. Symptoms vary for these diseases in an unpredictable manner. Some people may recover after a single attack. Some are in remission for years before suffering another unexpected attack. Others may face frequent hospitalizations and surgeries. In any case, the great challenge is dealing with something that cannot be foreseen—unpredictable attacks that may make it impractical to manage financial and other affairs for weeks at a time. Just like individuals with forms of MS characterized by unexpected exacerbations, those with Crohn's disease and ulcerative colitis may face unexpected short-term hospital stays when their conditions flare up. If you are living with one of these illnesses, you likely have your full mental faculties but may occasionally need the assistance of an agent on a short-term and unanticipated basis to handle routine (not major) matters.

If you have a flare-up or attack, you want your agent to assume control as soon as you are unable to do so; you also want control to revert to you as soon as you become able once more to handle your affairs. Springing powers are not designed to match these needs because your agent would periodically have to go through the process of demonstrating your disability and then recovery, thus hindering quick action to help you in the event of a flare-up and also potentially hindering your right to resume acting on your own behalf. In a worst-case scenario, implementing a springing power may mean that by the time your agent has legally demonstrated her ability to serve, you may already be in remission and again be able to handle your own affairs.

EXAMPLE • *Power of Attorney and Multiple Sclerosis*

Jane Smith has MS. She has long periods when she is fully capable of handling all financial, legal, and other matters that a durable power may cover. Although she uses a walking aide and struggles with fatigue, she is on top of all her financial, business, and other affairs. In fact, she continues to operate a lucrative design business, only she now does so out of a home office to make it easier to rest when she is fatigued. However, Jane's periods of activity are occasionally interrupted by brief periods of exacerbation lasting days or weeks when it is difficult or impossible for her cope without an agent's assistance. These exacerbations are unpredictable, and even the causes that trigger them are generally uncertain. If the appointment of the agent is effective immediately upon execution, unencumbered by the springing mechanism, the agent will be able to help during a short-term exacerbation or relapse. The agent can cede control back to Jane as soon as feasible, that is, as soon as the illness-related attack has passed. With a springing power, by the time the agent can legally demonstrate Jane's disability, the relapse will probably have subsided.

Another issue Jane faces is that, although she is fully competent to handle all her affairs, her mobility issues and fatigue often make it a chore to physically go to the bank. Although Jane has automated as many banking tasks as possible online, business issues demand her presence at the bank at least several times a week. Signing the typically proposed immediate (not springing) broad and general (covers everything) power of attorney would cause Jane to cede more control than she really wants to give an agent. This dilemma and similar circumstances can be addressed by the hybrid approach discussed in the next section.

HYBRID APPROACH BEST FOR SOME CHRONIC ILLNESSES

The answer to Jane's dilemma provides a creative and flexible approach that will benefit many people with chronic illness. It is an approach that maximizes the benefits of springing durable powers of attorney for those facing sporadic flare-ups or attacks. It is important to note that such hybridization must be approached carefully and only with the assistance of a professional well versed in the associated risks and benefits.

If you have a chronic illness but also have long periods when you are capable of handling all of your financial legal and tax matters, you don't want to lose control over your affairs during those periods. These periods may be interrupted by brief periods of exacerbations lasting days or weeks when it is difficult or impossible to cope without an agent's assistance. In most situations your agent will not have to make the major long-term decisions that an agent for someone suffering with Alzheimer's disease dementia will have to make. Major decisions can probably be deferred until you recover from a flare-up. (This obviously does not apply to individuals with significant and permanent dementia from AD or some other permanent disabling condition, who will never again be able to make decisions for themselves.)

As noted above, MS exacerbations are unpredictable, and there is no accurate way to assess what triggers them. This makes the generic springing mechanism a cumbersome tool that often creates more problems than it solves. An alternative is to consider using two separate powers of attorney to protect you while simultaneously preserving your independence.

The first document is a typical general durable power of attorney with springing provisions for agents. Should your disability increase to the degree an agent will have to operate on an ongoing basis, this broad power of attorney, similar to that used by estate planners generally, will be available. It includes a springing mechanism, with appropriate modifications that are tailored to address your specific illness. The sample clause below illustrates how this power can be tailored.

Sample Clause

"The Grantor shall be deemed disabled when Grantor is unable to manage Grantor's affairs and property effectively for a period anticipated being more than thirty (30) days [This duration was included to avoid triggering the power of any successor agent to act, as a result of a short-term exacerbation.] Disability may be determined to exist for reasons such as mental illness, mental deficiency, physical illness or disability, advanced age, chronic use of drugs, chronic intoxication, or for any other reason allowable by law. In addition to any other method allowed by law to determine disability, it shall be deemed conclusive proof that the Grant to the Alternate Agent is effective upon a sworn statement being executed by Grantor's attending neurologist."

The second document is a limited power of attorney, effective immediately with no springing provision. This power limits the agent's rights to those matters that might need addressing during a short-term flare-up or exacerbation. No power should be provided to make gifts, change beneficiary designations on insurance and retirement plans, sell real estate, etc. Those major decisions can wait until you recover from the short-term flare-up. This provides a secure option in the event the agent under a broad springing power is unable to help you (i.e., because of the difficulty and time required to demonstrate your disability). This approach does not cede powers that you should retain over your affairs for the foreseeable future and that your illness may never impact, yet it should facilitate quick assistance if needed. The purported protection some people believe a springing power provides (i.e., by limiting your agent's right to act until you are proven disabled) are unnecessary in this power of attorney because of the limitations on the rights granted. The same people could be named agents in both the general power discussed above, and this limited power, so there can be no conflict between the agents appointed under each.

COMMON ISSUES AFFECTING POWERS OF ATTORNEY

DIFFERENT TYPES OF POWERS YOU MIGHT SIGN

There are many different types of powers of attorney that should be considered. In most instances more than one type of power will be worth considering for optimal flexibility and protection. Care must be exercised, however, because each type of power presents its own unique risks and shortcomings.

Bank/Brokerage Firm Standard Form

The first and simplest step is to call your bank, mutual fund, and the brokerage houses where you have your primary accounts, and ask for their standard forms. These may be as simple as a 3 × 5 card on which you fill in the account name, account number, and the name of the person you want to be your agent. You will sign it at the bank or in front of a notary. This is an excellent step to take. If the bank has a power of attorney on file, it is most likely to readily accept that agent's signature without question. Just be certain that you implicitly trust the person you are naming in this capacity since the benefit of the "springing" power is not available in these instances.

Standard/Statutory State Preprinted Form

Another type of power of attorney is the standard form used in your state. Most states have one or perhaps two companies that print forms that lawyers, banks, and other financial institutions most commonly use in that state. These forms are often based on a state statutory power of attorney and, as such, should track the language of the state statute. Obtaining access to one of those forms (commonly, they can be purchased for a few dollars in an office supply store or legal supply house or are available online) can enable you to put in place a simple, basic level of protection. The powers of attorney in almost all instances must be notarized and, in many instances, someone should witness your signature as well.

These forms are typically one to four pages, relatively simple, widely accepted and recognized by all institutions, attorneys, etc., in the state. The key advantage that these forms have is that they are short, simple, inexpensive, and readily accepted. However, and this is an important caution, you should be certain to review the provisions of these forms with an attorney.

Comprehensive Power

Perhaps the most important type of power of attorney is an attorney drafted comprehensive durable power of attorney form tailored specifically for your circumstances. This is important because the standard forms lack many important provisions. Before retaining an attorney, make sure he or she is a specialist in the estate planning area. You should inquire whether the attorney understands the special provisions that should be in a comprehensive power of attorney and that the standard forms lack. These special provisions include the right to make gifts, the right to deal with the IRS, and more comprehensive power provisions. The right to make gifts is essential. Without specifically providing for the agent's right to make a gift, the IRS (under the laws of many states) will not accept the agent's gifts as binding for tax purposes. This can be very important because starting and continuing an aggressive gift program is an essential estate planning tool. The ability to continue this plan or program in the event of your disability could be essential to saving tens of thousands of estate tax dollars for your heirs. Specific and detailed authority to deal with the IRS is important. In the event of an IRS lien, whether mistakenly or appropriately placed on one of your accounts, it is essential that authority be given to the agent to deal with the Internal Revenue Service. Standard forms do not include such language, and this can create difficulties in the event of a disability. These are discussed in greater length later in this chapter.

Most comprehensive power of attorney forms are lengthy and contain broad detailed powers that grant the agent specific authority to deal with various types of situations. These include funding a revocable living trust to minimize or avoid probate, dealing with business matters, and other matters that the standard forms or your state's law may not address.

HOW MUCH AUTHORITY SHOULD AN AGENT BE GIVEN?

Deciding how much authority (and when) you should give your agent was discussed earlier in this chapter in the context of springing powers and crafting powers to fit your particular chronic illness. But this issue has broad implications beyond just the modifications discussed above that you might consider in light of your diagnosis. Powers of attorney are serious documents and can convey substantial authority, in the extreme enabling someone to change the entire dispositive scheme of the your estate plan and gift away all assets. If the grantor does not sufficiently trust someone to act in his or her best interest, other options should be considered.

EXAMPLE

An elderly widow's nearest living relative was a nephew she saw a few times a year around the holidays. She named the nephew as agent under a general power of attorney. The nephew, realizing that his elderly aunt had limited mobility and limited awareness, began to actively use her funds for his own benefit. By the time he was discovered and the powers were revoked, he had nearly wiped out his aunt's estate. By then his aunt was too elderly and infirm to pursue the matter and had insufficient funds to hire an attorney. The nephew was never taken to task for his actions.

KEY

> If there is no one who is 100 percent trustworthy, consider setting up a revocable living trust with a bank or trust company as cotrustee, or successor cotrustee. This will give you (the grantor) total control of assets and provide for professional management of your investments. Liability insurance, government regulations and audits, and internal controls, which all large institutions have, provide assurance that your assets will be safe. (See Chapter 12.)

POWER TO MAKE GIFTS

POWER OF AGENT TO MAKE GIFTS GENERALLY

If you are unable to sign and distribute checks or meet with a lawyer to plan more complex gifts (e.g., the transfer of part of the ownership of a family business), a power of attorney can authorize your agent to make gifts to people you designate and take other actions to minimize your estate tax. You can authorize your agent, as many form powers do, to make annual gifts up to the maximum amount permitted without any gift tax consequences. This can be quite a large amount. It includes $13,000 gifts in any year to as many different people as you want. If you have a score of nieces and nephews, that's big bucks. The $13,000 amount is the allowable figure for 2009, but because it is indexed for inflation, a larger limit may apply in later years. In addition, you can also give unlimited amounts for tuition and medical payments (i.e., these payments are not counted toward the $13,000 annual exclusion figure). If those same score of nieces and nephews are all in private colleges, you could theoretically gift millions over a short time. The power of your agent to make gifts can be a tremendous planning tool, but it can add up to significant sums.

EXAMPLE

A father began a regular gift program in which he and his wife join in making annual gifts of stock to each of their four children, their children's spouses, and their ten grandchildren. The gifts are each $24,000 in value, the maximum amount that can be given away each year without any gift tax being due, for a total of $432,000 [(4 + 4 + 10) × $12,000 × 2] based on the 2008 maximum gift limit of $12,000 per donee. The father falls ill in December and is unable to sign the necessary documents to make a transfer for the year so the couple makes no gifts in that year. The couple could incur an unnecessary additional estate tax cost of as much as $216,000 (assuming a 50 percent maximum rate, although the actual federal rate is lower) because this gift was not made. Had the father prepared an appropriate power of attorney, his agent may have been able to handle the paperwork necessary to make the gifts and eliminate this unnecessary estate tax burden. The figure would be higher if gifts for tuition and medical expenses were also made.

SHOULD YOU CURTAIL OR ELIMINATE GIFT POWERS IN LIGHT OF YOUR ILLNESS?

Most powers of attorney authorize agents to make gifts. The fatigue, cognitive impairment, or other symptoms of your illness may make it difficult for you to work at the same pace as previously. You may even have to cease working altogether. However, if employer-provided insurance coverage is lost, the out-of-pocket costs of treatment therapies is tremendous, often tens of thousands of dollars per year. Thus, the economic reality of your diagnosis may warrant their reconsideration of gift powers. Although a broad gift authority may have been appropriate before your diagnosis, it might be advisable (following a diagnosis of a chronic illness) to expressly prohibit gifts in order to preserve resources for your own uncertain future.

POWER TO MAKE GIFTS FOR MEDICAID PLANNING

For many people with a chronic illness, the opposite approach to gifts may be preferable. The only way to ascertain this is to consult with an elder law attorney. Gifts to reduce assets for Medicaid purposes, for example, are becoming more prevalent. Making a transfer to reduce your assets requires that the power of attorney have a broad gift power sufficient to give away all assets. If the clause is not sufficiently precise, governmental authorities will not respect the gifts. Such a power is so broad that it makes your power of attorney tantamount to a will in that it becomes your primary dispositive document.

This raises a host of risks and issues. One issue is that most state laws have very few requirements for the effectiveness of a power of attorney (perhaps a notary only, no witnesses, etc.). When a power becomes your primary dispositive document, more care should be taken to ensure that certain safeguards exist. Think of how dangerous this could be without such safeguards. What if a home health worker has you sign a power when you are not really cognizant of the impact or consequences of what you are doing? Planning in advance, perhaps funding a revocable trust with an institutional trustee, can avoid the risk and prevent much harm to your estate.

SPECIAL CONSIDERATIONS FOR NAMING AGENTS

Depending on the symptoms of your chronic disease, you will have to consider the availability and reliability of the agent you choose to name. In the event of a relapsing disease, will your agent be available quickly? If your disease progresses irreparably, will your agent have time to serve for an extended period of time? You may also want to consider exactly whom you are appointing to this position. You may have previously assumed it would be one person, but does your diagnosis change that? When you told your family and friends about your illness, how did they react? Were they supportive? Understanding? Did they fully comprehend the impact of your disease? These are only a few of the new issues you will need to consider when choosing a person who will serve on your behalf. It may be difficult not to choose someone who expects to be chosen, but you must select the agent who best understands the impact of your disease and who will best implement your wishes if you cannot.

You should name several alternate agents as a precaution in the event that the primary agent is unable or unwilling to take the necessary actions. This is especially important if your illness could result in your requiring help for a long period, even decades.

OTHER PROVISIONS TO CONSIDER

SHOULD YOUR AGENT BE GIVEN UNLIMITED POWER?

Your agent is generally authorized, among other things, to sign checks to pay for your medical care if you are hospitalized unexpectedly. Handling financial affairs, collecting dividend checks, selling stocks and bonds, and other basic financial transactions are also generally authorized. You may, however, wish to place restrictions on the scope of your agent's actions. This was discussed above in the context of how you might tailor your power of attorney to address an on-again, off-again illness, and in light of a springing power. Remember, in all instances, the documents you sign must accomplish your goals and deal with your unique circumstances.

For example, you might limit your agent to permit only the payment of certain emergency expenses. You could expressly permit, or deny, your agent the right to sell your home or other real estate assets. Gift giving always warrants careful attention. The form provided in this book does not place any restrictions on your agent. If you are concerned, there are several options you should evaluate. Suppose, at some point, you realize that you may have selected the wrong person as agent. If you do not feel enough trust and confidence in this person, you may be motivated to restrict his or her powers or consider naming a different person as agent. In some cases, although it is cumbersome from an administrative perspective and your attorney might even advise against it, you might have to appoint two co-agents to act together. The requirement for two signatures to approve any action may give you the assurance you want of neither agent violating your wishes or taking advantage of you. If you don't have anyone else to name, you might need a revocable living trust with an institution as a trustee or as cotrustee. (See Chapter 10.)

BUSINESS POWERS

The general discussion of business powers of attorney presented above can also be reviewed for the purpose of setting limits, making modifications, or consideration of special nuances. If you have a business, such as a home-based business, which is not a corporation, partnership, or other entity, your agent under your power of attorney can be authorized to handle business matters for you. If your business is a corporation, partnership, limited liability company, or other type of entity, your power of attorney may not authorize you to take action for that entity. The entity itself must do that. If your business is a corporation, the shareholders should appoint people to serve as directors. The directors will generally appoint officers. Sometimes, but not always, all officers will be approved in the corporate minutes to sign bank accounts or handle other transactions. If you have these issues, don't take chances. In all such cases, consult with a corporate or business attorney and be certain that disability issues are addressed. A shareholder agreement and buy-sell agreement should be reviewed or, if you don't have them, obtain them. If you operate a professional practice as a solo practitioner, you may be obligated to prepare a special limited power of attorney that provides a colleague or other licensed professional the right and obligation to manage your practice during an illness or disability and to transition your practice in the event of a permanent disability or death.

EXAMPLE

Dana Jones is an attorney. She lives with her partner, Sarah, who is a clothing designer. Dana cannot name Sarah to handle legal matters for her law practice during a period that Dana cannot act because Sarah is not an attorney. Dana therefore signs a limited (special) durable (effective during disability) power of attorney to her colleague John Smith naming him as agent to manage her practice if she cannot. Dana gives Sarah a general (broad and all encompassing) durable power of attorney to handle all her other affairs. To avoid any conflict between Sarah and John, Dana provides in the general power to Sarah one restriction—Sarah cannot make decisions concerning Dana's law practice. Furthermore, to better coordinate the activities of her two agents, Dana specifically authorizes Sarah to loan money to her law practice if necessary to help it through a period of time when she cannot work (e.g., to hire staff to cover for her).

POWER TO DEAL WITH THE TAX AUTHORITIES

Dealing with the IRS can be an important matter. If you are unable to act, someone might need to sign a tax return for you (Form 1040 personal income tax return), or your home business (e.g., sales tax return), handle a tax audit, or address a lien erroneously placed on your accounts. This is an essential part of your planning. Your power of attorney should include:

❖ Specific rights to deal with IRS (federal), state (state income tax, sales tax if you have a business), and local (e.g., town property tax) tax matters.

❖ Include your Social Security number in your power of attorney to facilitate your agent's work with tax authorities.

❖ Authorize your agent to sign any additional documents required for him or her to work with the various tax authorities, including but not limited to the IRS Form 2848 discussed below.

In addition to authorizing your agent to deal with the IRS and handle other tax matters in your power of authority, it can be helpful in certain circumstances to sign a special IRS form for this purpose. Always check with your accountant before doing this. Form 2848 is the IRS power of attorney that authorizes someone to act on your behalf with respect to tax matters. If you are audited by the IRS, one of the first things your attorney or accountant will request is that you sign a copy of Form 2848, "Power of Attorney and Declaration of Representative." This form must be on file with the IRS before any IRS agent will communicate with your accountant. Although the form is quite simple, there are a number of points and practical suggestions that can save time and reduce problems. It's always best to sign a number of extra copies of Form 2848 and have your accountant keep them in your file. A supply of extra signed forms will eliminate the need for your accountant to prepare new forms for your signature, especially if you make them applicable to a number of years and all your tax returns.

Read the form before you sign. You do not need to authorize your accountant to represent you for years and types of taxes other than what the particular audit is about. This is one way for you to control what your accountant is doing before seeking your approval. While this may be appropriate for most taxpayers, depending on your circumstances, a broader grant of authority may be preferable. There are boxes to check to tell the IRS where to send communication concerning the audit. Make sure both you and your accountant get copies. You don't want your accountant to indicate that correspondence should go only to him or her. You want copies sent to you (or your agent under your power of attorney), so you (or your agent) can monitor what is going on. Be careful with respect to the authorization to receive the payment of any refund. Only under a few special circumstances should you ever check the box authorizing your accountant to receive any refund check. Note that these boxes are sometimes checked by accountants without consultation with the taxpayer(s) signing the form. With this in mind, consider expressly directing any refunds to you or your agent.

COMPENSATING YOUR AGENT

Generally, agents under a power of attorney are not compensated for their activities. However, you may want to consider whether your illness and the scope of activities your agent may be required to engage in on your behalf for a significant length of time warrants compensation. Should you compensate an agent who has to serve for a long time or at frequent intervals? If you do include a compensation clause, will you take into account when and how often your agent is likely to serve? You probably do not want to undercompensate an agent (even a family member) who serves full time for many months or years, as this may lead to less than full attention being paid to your financial issues. A common initial reaction is that a friend or family member doesn't need to get paid to help out. The reality is that your agent (at least those who take the job seriously) may have to handle paying your bills, filing your tax returns, managing your home repairs, and more for decades. That level of commitment should not go unpaid. If your agent becomes resentful of the time involved, or if the agent's spouse or partner becomes resentful of the commitment, compensation may alleviate some of the associated problems. Often it is not even an issue of money: Your agent may be more comfortable financially than you are and may simply appreciate an acknowledgement of the efforts involved.

If you determine that compensation is warranted, compensation provisions should be tailored to the unique circumstances of your chronic illness. The first question you must address is how to set the amount of compensation. Some attorneys use state law compensation for a trustee as a gauge for calculating an agent's compensation under a power of attorney. While that may work, it is a technical approach and legal advice will be necessary to interpret and implement such a provision. Moreover, while this type of compensation might make sense for someone with ALS or Alzheimer's disease, for whom the agent shoulders all responsibilities, it might be excessive for someone with Parkinson's disease, who may need help with complex issues and some paperwork, but can still handle many affairs without assistance.

For someone with MS who has periodic attacks but thereafter regains the ability to manage his or her own affairs, an agent's involvement may be sporadic and of short duration. But for some MS patients, attacks may recur several times a year, and this creates the need for additional assistance. Compensation based on statutory trustee fees would be impractical (prorating a statutory percentage of assets for a week long period) and may not be sufficient to cover the emergent and recurring nature of the agent's involvement. Thus, some stated minimum compensation each time the agent acts may be preferable. This type of compensation could change with changing circumstances. That is, if the agent begins to operate on a permanent basis compensation changes. For the majority of MS clients, a two-tier compensation structure might be advisable. Compensation under the limited special power of attorney discussed above could be provided as follows:

Sample Clause

> "In the event an agent acts hereunder, the agent shall be compensated at the rate of $X/week for any week in which the agent provides any services or acts hereunder, up to a maximum of Six (6) weeks in any given year. Compensation has been provided at a level to encourage the agent's involvement, and in recognition of the potential for having to act with little notice and at inconvenient times."

In plain English, this can be translated as "I want to reward and motivate the agents to act, even though she is a close friend or family member who would act without compensation." Even the occurrence of several exacerbations during a year should readily be covered by the six-week period. But this cap will prevent the intended reward from becoming an unreasonable expense if a permanent issue arises. The second tier would be conpensation as a trustee discussed above.

STATE-SPECIFIC ISSUES; RECORDING

As noted earlier in this chapter, it is important to address any particular issues of state law. In some states, particular attention should be paid to laws that limit who you may name as an attorney to certain close relatives In other states it may be advisable to file the power of attorney of record, as the example below illustrates.

EXAMPLE

Dennis Frank has Parkinson's disease. As his disease has progressed, he has stayed in control of all his legal and financial matters, but he now recognizes that he will need help. His only living family members, a son and aunt, are not appropriate to name as agents. His aunt is quite elderly, and his son, to Dennis' disappointment, has not been of much help. Dennis decides to name Jeff Green, his longtime CPA, as agent. In order to protect Jeff from a claim by Dennis' son, Dennis has an independent attorney prepare and supervise the signing of the power at a time when Jeff Green is not in the attorney's office. Upon his attorney's recommendation, Dennis has the power of attorney recorded in the local county clerk's office. By making the appointment a matter of public record, Dennis has made it easier for Jeff to help him. The manner in which the power of attorney was recorded also makes it clear that Dennis was aware of the grant of the power to Jeff, and that Jeff was not in any manner hiding this appointment from Dennis' disenfranchised son.

RELATIONSHIP OF POWER OF ATTORNEY RELATED TO OTHER ESTATE PLANNING DOCUMENTS

❖   **Revocable living trust.** A revocable living trust is not a substitute for a durable power of attorney. This is because a revocable living trust can only provide control to a trustee over the assets that have been transferred to the trust. A power of attorney, however, if broadly written, can give an agent access to all of your assets that have not been transferred to your living trust. Since a durable power of attorney immediately terminates on death, it can never be considered a substitute for a will or trust arrangement.

❖   **Will.** Since a durable power of attorney terminates on your death, it can never be considered a substitute for a will or trust arrangement. Thus, a will and/or revocable living trust (which becomes irrevocable on your death), are generally essential since both address the disposition of assets after death, whereas the power of attorney will not. However, many powers give the agent broad enough powers to give away all assets, so the power of attorney begins to look like a will substitute, a situation that raises a range of concerns and issues.

❖ **Living will/health care proxy.** A financial/legal power of attorney should not be combined with a power of attorney for health care matters (a health care proxy). Many state laws, in fact, prohibit such combinations. Regardless of state law, the decisions are very different and often, the people named as agents in one document are different from those named as agents to the other. Effort should be made to avoid enabling your health care agent to make decisions concerning your health that could also affect financial issues over which the same agent has control.

CHAPTER SUMMARY

A power of attorney, or several types of powers of attorney, could be the most important document you sign to ensure that your financial, legal, tax, and certain other matters are properly addressed. If properly planned, powers can provide you with the maximum control over your affairs, while assuring support and protection when you need it. These are serious documents that can involve your giving tremendous authority to the person(s) you appoint as your agent(s). They should not be treated as "standard" but should be carefully thought out and tailored to your needs.

PREPARED BY

_____:

LAWYER-NAME, Esq.

IMMEDIATE, GENERAL, AND DURABLE

POWER OF ATTORNEY

KNOW ALL PERSONS BY THESE PRESENTS, that I *CLIENTNAME (the "Grantor") (Social Security Number: *SOCIALSEC), residing at *CLIENT-ADDRESS, being of the age of majority under the laws of *STATENAME, and of sufficient capacity to conduct my business and financial affairs, in order to provide for management of Grantor's financial, legal and related, affairs in a more orderly fashion, hereby declare as follows:

1. Appointment of Agent. Grantor hereby makes, constitutes, and appoints ("Grant") *AGENT1-NAME residing at *AGENT-1ADDRESS, as Grantor's true and lawful Attorney-in-Fact and agent (the "Agent") for Grantor and in Grantor's name, place, and stead and for Grantor's benefit, or any alternate appointed in accordance with the provisions of this Power of Attorney (the "Agent").

2. Alternate Agent.

a. If *AGENT1-NAME is unwilling or unable to act as Agent, Grantor appoints the first person able and willing to serve from the following list, as Grantor's Agent (the "Alternate Agent"):

i. *AGENT2-NAME, who resides at *AGENT-2ADDRESS.

ii. *AGENT3-NAME, who resides at *AGENT-3ADDRESS.

iii. *AGENT4-NAME, who resides at *AGENT-4ADDRESS.

b. Such person shall serve as Grantor's Agent. The timing of the appointment of the Alternate Agent shall be governed by the provision below, "Effective Date." Any rights or powers granted to the Agent are granted to the Alternate Agent, unless specifically provided to the contrary.

3. Direction to Agent to Support Grantor and Named Persons.

a. The Agent is hereby authorized and directed to perform all acts reasonable and necessary to maintain Grantor's customary standard of living: to provide living quarters by purchase, lease, or other arrangement, or by payment of the operating costs of Grantor's existing living quarters, including interest, amortization payments, repairs, taxes, and so forth; to provide for the retention and payment of reasonably necessary domestic help for the maintenance and operation of Grantor's household; home health assistance and companion care if necessary; to finance or arrange for the purchase of other necessaries, including but not limited to clothing, transportation, entertainment, and incidentals; and to provide medical care, including the payment for experimental and novel medications and treatments if approved by Grantor's health care agent.

b. The Agent is further authorized and directed to provide for the health, education, support, and maintenance of Grantor's spouse, and Grantor's children (whether or not such children are minors or dependents, and even if above the age of majority), in accordance with an ascertainable standard as defined in Code Section 2041 and the Regulations thereunder. Grantor recognizes that such transfers to or for the benefit of persons other than Grantor may constitute gifts and authorizes that such transfers be permitted and that such transfers not be restricted by the provisions below under the caption "Gifts." These support payments, however, shall not be in excess of those Grantor has traditionally paid, and shall give consideration to any worsening of Grantor's health status and the impact of that on Grantor's finances.

c. Notwithstanding anything in this provision to the contrary, no Agent may exercise any power granted in this provision, or elsewhere in this Power of Attorney, in a manner that would cause any of Grantor's assets or estate to be taxable in the estate of any Agent. The foregoing sentence shall serve as an affirmative restriction and limitation on the right of any Agent acting hereunder.

d. Comment: Add provision and details concerning support of any pets.

4. Powers of Agent. The Agent is hereby granted all the powers and rights necessary to effect Grantor's wishes, including, in addition to any power authorized by the laws of *STATENAME for an agent, the following:

a. <u>General Financial Matters.</u>

i. Request, ask, demand, sue for, recover, sell, buy, collect, forgive, receive, and hold money, debts, dues, commercial paper, checks, drafts, accounts, deposits, legacies, bequests, devises, notes, interests, stocks, bonds, certificates of deposit, annuities, pension and retirement benefits, insurance proceeds, any and all documents of title; choose in action, personal and real property, intangible and tangible property and property rights; and demand whatsoever, liquidated or unliquidated, as now are or may become owned by, or due, owing, payable, or belonging to Grantor, or in which Grantor has or may hereafter acquire interest.

ii. Agent may use and take all lawful means and equitable and legal remedies, procedures, and writs in Grantor's name for the collection and recovery of the above; and may adjust, sell, compromise, and agree for the same; and to make, execute, and deliver for Grantor, on Grantor's behalf and in Grantor's name, all endorsements, acceptances, releases, receipts, or other sufficient discharges for the same.

b. Business.

i. Conduct, engage in and transact any lawful business of any nature on Grantor's behalf and in Grantor's name. Maintain, improve, invest, manage, insure, lease, or encumber; and in any manner deal with any real, personal, tangible, or intangible property, or any interest in them, that Grantor now owns or may acquire (or that an Agent hereunder may acquire), in Grantor's name and for Grantor's benefit, upon such terms and conditions as Agent shall deem proper.

ii. Conduct or participate in any business of any nature for Grantor and in Grantor's name; execute partnership agreements and amendments thereto; incorporate, reorganize, merge, consolidate, recapitalize, sell, liquidate, or dissolve any business; elect or employ officers, directors, and agents. Carry out the provisions of any agreement for the sale of any business interest or the stock therein; and exercise voting rights with respect to stock, either in person or by proxy; and exercise stock options.

c. Social Security and Government Benefits.

i. The Agent may apply to any governmental agency for any benefit or government obligation to which Grantor may be entitled, including but not limited to Social Security, Medicare, Medicaid, and Veterans benefits if applicable.

ii. The Agent may endorse any drafts or checks made payable to Grantor from any such agency and to serve as a representative payee for Social Security or other governmental payments. The Agent is expressly authorized to execute vouchers on Grantor's behalf for reimbursements properly payable to Grantor by the United States government or any agency thereof or any state agency. The Agent is expressly authorized to change Grantor's address for the purpose of receiving checks, mail, or other matters from the Social Security Administration or any other governmental agency.

d. Contract, Real Estate, and Other Matters.

i. The Agent may exercise or perform any act, power, duty, right, or obligation that Grantor now has, or may acquire, including the legal right, power, or capacity to exercise or perform in connection with, arising from, or relating to any person or property, real or personal, tangible or intangible, or matter whatsoever.

ii. This includes, without limiting the foregoing, the right to execute a deed or security agreement; to release a security agreement; to enter into a lease, option, mortgage or similar arrangement; to enter into a contract of sale and to sell or purchase any real, personal, tangible, or intangible property on Grantor's behalf.

iii. Comment: Consider listing specific properties which the agent may sell or act upon. In addition, consider listing any property which you do not want the agent to sell or act upon. The aforementioned powers shall apply, by way of example and not limitation, to the property (properties) located at *CLIENT-ADDRESS #and *OTHER PROPERTY.

e. Securities and Investments.

i. Make, receive, sign, endorse, acknowledge, deliver, and possess documents of title, bonds, debentures, checks, drafts, stocks, proxies, or warrants, relating to accounts or deposits, or certificates of deposit, other debts and obligations, and such other instruments in writing of whatever kind and nature as may be necessary or proper in the exercise of the rights and powers herein granted.

ii. Sell, or purchase any and all shares of stocks, bonds, or other securities now or later belonging to Grantor that may be issued by any association, trust, or corporation, whether private or public; and make, execute, and deliver any assignment, or assignments, of any such shares of stocks, bonds, or other securities.

f. Motor Vehicles.

Apply for any certificate of title, ownership, or license; endorse and transfer title regarding any automobile, motorcycle, or other motor vehicle or boat.

g. Legal Actions.

i Settle, adjust, compromise, or submit to arbitration any accounts, claims, debts, demands, disputes, or other matters between Grantor and any other person or entity, or which concern any property, right, title, interest, or estate. Begin, prosecute, enforce, abandon, defend, or settle all claims or judicial or administrative proceedings.

ii. Execute and file documents to toll any statute of limitations. Grantor recognizes that the inclusion of the latter phrase may serve to prevent the tolling of a statute of limitations or other deadline which would otherwise be tolled pending Grantor's disability.

h. Retirement, IRA, and Other Benefit Plans and Beneficiary Designations.

i. Comment: Be certain that you understand the consequences of this paragraph. Changing beneficiary designations on retirement and pension accounts can have profound tax consequences, can change the dispositive scheme of the largest asset in your estate.

ii. Redeem, borrow, amend, cancel, pledge, surrender, alter, or change the beneficiary of any retirement, benefit, pension plan or other plan or account having a beneficiary designation form.

iii. However, this power may not be exercised by any agent who is a beneficiary (or spouse of a beneficiary) in a manner which disproportionately (as compared to the consequences of the beneficiary designation existing prior to the agent institute change) benefits such agent (or the spouse of such agent).

iv. Designate to the extent Grantor could one or more persons (including trusts) as designated beneficiaries of any such plan. Select any pay-out rate or election permitted to Grantor.

i. Employment of Accountants, Advisers, and Others.

Employ and compensate investment advisers, banks, accountants, expert witness, attorneys, real estate and other brokers, and other professionals or assistants to same, whom the Agent reasonably deems necessary. To cause such persons to prepare reports or analysis, and to act in reasonable reliance upon same, and to furnish any third party Agent believes necessary or appropriate such reports or analysis. There shall be no restriction on the Agent hiring or not hiring the advisers which grantor used.

j. Safe Deposit Box.

Have access at any time or times to any safe deposit box rented by Grantor, or for which Grantor is a co-tenant; remove all or any part of the contents thereof, and surrender or relinquish any safe deposit box. No institution in which any safe deposit box may be located shall incur any liability to Grantor or Grantor's estate as a result of permitting the Agent to exercise the powers herein granted.

k. Gifts.

The Agent shall not have any authority to make gifts.

l. Transfer of Property to Trust.

With respect to a revocable living trust for the benefit of Grantor the Agent may convey, transfer or assign any cash, real estate or other tangible or intangible property in which Grantor shall own any interest to the trustee or trustees of any trust that Grantor may have created during Grantor's lifetime, provided that such trust is subject to Grantor's power of revocation.

m. Postal Matters.

To execute any documents necessary or appropriate to securing a postal box, changing or correcting a postal mailing address, and making payments for same. By way of example and not limitation, this power shall expressly include the right to redirect mail from any former residence or post-office box to a new address or post-office box which the Agent reasonably believes will facilitate the management of Grantor's assets, tax, legal and other matters. Any third party, including but not limited to the United States government and any agency thereof, are directed to adhere to such requests of the Agent and are indemnified and held harmless for same.

n. Bond.

No bond or security of any kind shall be required in any jurisdiction of any Agent acting hereunder. If any bond is required by law, statute or rule of court, no sureties shall be required thereon. However, if any Agent deems it appropriate in such Agent's discretion to obtain a bond, such bond may be paid pursuant to the powers granted hereunder.

o. Insurance.

i. Make, receive, sign, endorse, acknowledge, deliver, and possess insurance policies. Execute any forms to change ownership or beneficiaries of any life insurance policy on Grantor's life.

ii. However, new beneficiaries may include only: Authorized Donees, a trust for which Authorized Donees are the primary beneficiaries, a corporation or partnership in which Grantor is a shareholder or partner, another shareholder or partner in a corporation or partnership in which Grantor is a shareholder or partner, Grantor's estate, or any trust of which Grantor is a grantor, trustee, or beneficiary.

5. Powers Relating to Tax Matters.

a. In addition to, and not by way of limitation upon, any other powers conferred upon Grantor's Agent herein, Grantor grants to the Agent full power and authority to do, take, and perform each and every act and thing which is reasonably required, proper, or necessary to be done in connection with the following:

b. Receiving and depositing to any of Grantor's bank or brokerage accounts any refund checks with respect to any tax filing. Preparing, signing, and filing joint or separate income tax returns, declarations, or estimated tax for any year or years, as provided in Treasury Regulation Section 1.6012-1(a)(5) and Treasury Regulation Section 25.6019-1(d), or otherwise.

c. Prepare, sign, and file joint or separate gift, or other tax returns, declarations, or estimated tax for any year or years, including by way of example, those with respect to gifts made by Grantor, or by Grantor's Agent on Grantor's behalf, for any year or years; consent to any gift and to utilize any gift-splitting provision or other tax election.

d. Dealing with the Internal Revenue Service and any federal, state, local, and foreign tax authority concerning any gift, estate, inheritance, income, or other tax, and any audit or investigation of same. Prepare, sign and file any claim for refund of any tax; execute any extension or waiver of tax.

e. The powers granted hereunder shall include, by way of example and not limitation, the power to do all acts that could be authorized by Grantor having properly executed a Form 2848, "Power of Attorney and Declaration of Representative," granting the broadest powers provided therein to the Agent, the power to represent Grantor in any federal, state, local, or foreign tax matter, to perform all acts that Grantor could perform relating thereto.

f. Prepare and file Form 56, "Notice Concerning Fiduciary Relationship," or any similar form, for purposes of directing tax and other correspondence, notices and information to a new address which the Agent deems appropriate. I expressly state that it is my intent that the Agent acting under this Power of Attorney shall be deemed a "fiduciary" for the purposes of the filing of Form 56, or any similar form.

6. Compensation of Agent. Any Agent or Alternate Agent hereunder shall be entitled to reasonable compensation for the services rendered. A bill estimating the hours spent, services performed and charges paid, shall be provided to any Alternate Agent acting hereunder with such Agent. It shall be deemed reasonable compensation for the Agent to be paid in a manner similar to that provided for a trustee to be compensated under applicable state law for the investment and liquid assets (e.g., excluding residential real estate, but including investment real estate if any) that the Agent has authority over. In the event of a short term flare-up, exacerbation or other emergency in which the Agent shall act in an emergent basis for a short period of time Grantor recognizes that compensation reflective of the time and effort over that short duration may be more reasonable.

7. Cooperation With Health Care Agent.

a. If Grantor has executed a separate Living Will, Health Care Proxy, or Durable Power of Attorney For Medical Decisions, or a similar form or document appointing any person or entity to serve as Grantor's health care agent, Grantor requests that Grantor's Agent appointed herein cooperate with such health care agent and keep such health care agent reasonably advised of any financial matters relating to Grantor's health care. To the extent possible, Agent should abide by such health care agent's decisions and actions concerning Grantor's health care and the matters covered in such documents named above, and should assist in providing financial resources reasonable and necessary to implement such decisions.

8. Disability of Grantor. This Power of Attorney shall not be affected by Grantor's subsequent disability as principal. Grantor does hereby so provide, it being Grantor's intention that all powers conferred upon the Agent herein shall remain at all times in full force and effect, notwithstanding Grantor's subsequent incapacity, disability, or any uncertainty with regard thereto.

9. Third Party Reliance.

a. Third parties may rely upon the representations of the Agent for all matters relating to any power granted to the Agent, and no person who may act in reliance upon the representations of the Agent or the authority granted to the Agent shall incur any liability to the Grantor or Grantor's estate as a result of permitting the Agent to exercise such power.

b. Any third party may rely on a duly executed counterpart of this instrument, or a copy thereof, as fully and completely as if such third party had received the original of this instrument. Any third party may rely on the authority of any Alternate Agent when such Alternate Agent presents an original executed copy of this Power of Attorney. Such third party need not request proof, other than an affidavit of the Alternate Agent, under oath, that any prior named Agent is unable or unwilling to serve in such capacity.

10. Approval and Indemnification of Agent. Grantor hereby approves and confirms all acts performed by Grantor's Agent on Grantor's behalf. Grantor hereby confirms all that the Agent shall do or cause to be done, by virtue of this Power of Attorney. The Grantor hereby agrees to indemnify and hold harmless the Agent for any actions taken, or not taken, by the Agent, when the Agent acted in good faith and was not guilty of fraud, gross negligence, or willful misconduct, only for matters in this document.

11. Waiver of Conflicts for Agent and Successor Agent. No Agent or successor Agent shall be disqualified from acting in such capacity as a result of having an interest in any assets, business, investment or endeavor in which Grantor also has an interest, and over which Agent may have authority to act, and may act upon, hereunder.

12. HIPAA Provisions.

a. The Grantor expressly authorizes any Agent or successor to request, obtain, receive, and inspect any and all information including private health information ("PHI") that encompasses solely Grantor's medical bills and related information ("Bills"), and to sign whatever authorizations for release of any Bills which may be required by Grantor's Agent or any third party providers or others, and to waive any rights Grantor may have for breach of confidentiality for the release of such information to the Agent or successor Agent.

b. In no event shall the provisions herein give the Agent or successor Agent hereunder any powers to make medical or health care decisions for me. These rights and powers are granted solely with respect to the implementation and conducting of the rights and powers granted herein, including by way of example and not limitation, reviewing and paying bills.

c. The Agent and Successor Agent shall be treated as Grantor would with regard to the use and dissemination of Grantor's Bills. This authority applies to any information governed by the Health Insurance Portability and Accountability Act of 1996 ("HIPAA"), 42 USC 130d and 45 CFR 160-164. Grantor specifically authorizes any physician, dentist, health care professional, medical provider, health plan, hospital, clinic, laboratory, pharmacy or other covered health care provider, any insurance company and the Medical Information Bureau Inc., or any other health care organization that has provided treatment or services to Grantor, or that has paid for or is seeking payment from Grantor for such services to give, disclose and release to the Grantor's Agent and successor Agent all of Grantor's Bills. The authority given to Grantor's Agent and successor Agents has no expiration date and shall expire only in the event that Grantor revokes the authority in writing and delivers it to Grantor's health care provider.

13. Effective Date.

a. The Grant to the Agent (not the Alternate Agents) shall take effect on the date hereof.

The Grant to an Alternate Agent shall take effect only in the event that the prior named Agent or Alternate Agent is unable or unwilling to Act.

14. Construction.

a. This instrument is to be construed and interpreted as a durable general power of attorney. The enumeration of specific items, rights, acts, or powers herein is not intended to nor does it limit or restrict, and is not to be construed or interpreted as limiting or restricting, the general powers herein granted to the Agent.

b. Should any provision or power in this document not be enforceable, such enforceability shall not affect the enforceability of the rest of this document. Any such provision is not enforceable shall be deemed severable and all other provisions shall remain enforceable and shall be interpreted in a manner that as closely as feasible implements Grantor's original intent hereunder.

c. Any references to the "Code" or any Sections of the Code are references to the Internal Revenue Code of 1986 and shall include any successor or amended Code, statute, or applicable Treasury Regulation.

d. Captions, titles, and section numbers (and letter designations) are inserted for convenience only and should not be read to broaden or limit the scope of any provision. Gender, singular or plural, shall be interpreted as the context requires.

15. State Law.

i. This instrument is executed in the state of *STATE-EXECUTION, but and is delivered in the state of *STATENAME ("State"), and the laws of *STATENAME shall govern all questions as to the validity of this power and the construction of its provisions. It is Grantor's intention, however, that this power of attorney be exercisable in any other state or jurisdiction in which Grantor may at any time have property, business, or other dealings. The Agent is, notwithstanding anything herein to the contrary, granted the right to exercise any of the rights and powers available under the laws of the State.

16. Signature.

a. **IN WITNESS WHEREOF,** I have hereunto set my hand and seal this *DAY of *MONTH, *YEAR, acknowledging that I have read and understood the powers and rights herein granted and that I voluntarily chose to make the Grant.

Grantor/Principal

_____

*CLIENTNAME

Witness 1:   Name:_____

Address:_____

Signature:_____

Witness 2:   Name:_____

Address:_____

Signature:_____

State of *STATE-EXECUTION

          SS:

County of *COUNTYNAME

On this *DAY of *MONTH, *YEAR, I, a Notary Public in the State of *STATE-EXECUTION, certify that before me personally appeared *CLIENTNAME, who resides at *CLIENT-ADDRESS, and who I am satisfied based on presentation of a *STATENAME driver's license, is the person named in and who executed the within Power of Attorney, and who acknowledged under oath, and to my satisfaction, that the execution of the Power of Attorney by Grantor was done voluntarily for the uses and purposes therein expressed, and that Grantor, signed, sealed, and delivered the Power of Attorney as Grantor's act and deed. The execution of this Power of Attorney by the Grantor was done in my presence and in the presence of both witnesses above, each of whom signed their names in my presence and in Grantor's presence.

_____

Notary Public, State of *STATE-EXECUTION

My commission expires on: _____ ____, 200___

CHAPTER 6

Ensuring Access to Your Medical Records

HIPAA

Introduction to HIPAA

HIPAA is the affectionate acronym for the Health Insurance Portability and Accountability Act of 1996. HIPAA, as amended (it takes multiple efforts to perfect such complexity), protects your rights to your medical information, legally designated as "protected health information" or PHI. HIPAA was enacted to ensure you access to your medical information while simultaneously preventing others who should not have access to it from obtaining it. HIPAA rules have broad implications affecting a wide range of personal, estate planning, and business transactions.

WHY HIPAA MATTERS

HIPAA regulations determine how and to whom your medical information should be disclosed, and it is vitally important to understand these regulations and how they might affect you and people who have a vested interest in your health status. If, for example, you have a flare-up or go for surgery, does your daughter-in-law have the right to see your patient chart to monitor your care? If you're a trustee on your own revocable living trust, can your successor trustee take over in the event you deteriorate to a point where you cannot reasonably serve as your own trustee? And does this individual have the right to view any medical information about you? If you have a partner in an accounting practice, chances are you and your partner may have discussed contingency plans if your cognitive issues reach a level that makes it necessary for your partner to take over the practice. If your health status deteriorates, how can your partner obtain the requisite physician letter mandated in your shareholders' agreement to demonstrate your incompetence and thus trigger the buy-out of your interests? HIPAA needs to be addressed in all of these and many other common situations.

What a Medical Provider ("Covered Entity") Must Do to Protect You

Despite our society's current obsession with political correctness, most people with a chronic illness (or a loved one with a chronic illness) know the harsh non-PC reality of living in a world that is not always understanding or tolerant of chronic illness and those who are affected by it. Many people, in fact, including employers and others who may have the power to affect your life and livelihood can be ignorant, fearful, even antagonistic, to those with chronic illnesses. For this reason alone, you are not likely to want your private medical information disclosed, and you have the right to restrict disclosure.

Under HIPAA regulations, any organization (health plan, health care provider, or health clearinghouse) that routinely handles private health information in any capacity is probably characterized as a "covered entity" and all covered entities must provide information to their patients about their privacy rights and how their PHI can be used (notice of privacy practices). A covered entity must adopt clear and appropriate privacy policies and procedures for its practice, hospital, or plan. It must train its workforce to understand its privacy procedures and must designate a privacy officer responsible for ensuring that privacy procedures are adopted and followed. A covered entity must also adopt adequate security procedures for patient records containing individually identifiable private health information. Because medical practices fall under the classification of covered entity, even your doctor cannot disclose your health status to your employer or others without your authorization.

WHEN INFORMATION CAN BE DISCLOSED

Your otherwise protected health information should be disclosed for medical treatment, payment, and health care operations (no authorization or release is needed). Your medical information should be disclosed to you at your request. This is important because prior to HIPAA, a patchwork of state and local rules governed the release of health information, and your right to access your own medical records was not always assured. Your HIPAA personal representative (an agent selected by you and discussed in detail below) should also have access to your protected health information. A court can also order disclosure of your medical information. This can occur if, for example, someone tries to have a guardian appointed for you (a process you can likely avoid by taking the planning precautions in this book). The secretary of the Department of Health and Human Services can access health information for enforcement purposes.

WHEN INFORMATION MAY NOT BE DISCLOSED

If your physician, neurologist, or other health care professional believes that the disclosure of your health information might endanger your life, jeopardize your physical safety, or cause you or another person (e.g., someone else mentioned in your records) substantial harm, they can refuse in their professional judgment to disclose the information.

WHAT INFORMATION CAN BE DISCLOSED

Not all information has to be disclosed. Medical providers are only supposed to disclose the minimum information necessary to achieve the purpose of the requested disclosure. This can be an important safeguard of your confidentiality, but it might also prove to be a hindrance to your HIPAA personal representative. In part, what is disclosed will depend on the policies of the particular physician (or more broadly, covered entity as defined above). What is disclosed will also depend on the language you put in the legal documents authorizing someone to obtain disclosure of your medical records. To protect and limit the scope of what is disclosed, you should clearly delineate in any document you execute the specific purpose of the disclosure and what information should not be disclosed. Consider your unique situation and evolving circumstances when deciding what should or should not be disclosed.

EXAMPLE

If you are seeking to ensure that one of your adult children can help you with medical decisions, you may expressly want no limits imposed on what access this person has to your health information. In such a situation, a broad authorization to release all of your protected health information should be stated. Be careful with "standard" authorization forms. Just like the issues discussed in the preceding chapter on "standard" powers of attorney, generic forms related to health information can be quite dangerous. Standard forms for the release of your private health information may be too broad or too narrow, depending on your objectives. In some instances you may want extremely narrow disclosures. For example, the medical practice you work with might want assurance that your chronic illness won't negatively impact your ability to practice medicine. It is certainly reasonable for your colleagues to receive a letter from your attending neurologist that your illness won't adversely impact your practicing. On the other hand, an excessively broad grant of authority to access your medical information could result in disclosures of personal information way beyond what is necessary and appropriate. You certainly don't need the nursing staff discussing your MRI results by the water cooler. So to avoid abuses of your privacy, any document you sign should appropriately and reasonably restrict who should have access to your information and what information should be disclosed.

HOW TO GET INFORMATION DISCLOSED

As explained above, a medical provider ("covered entity") cannot disclose your protected health information (PHI) without your authorization. There are some exceptions to this policy, but HIPAA ensures that general access to your health information is strictly limited. You, as a patient, have the right to authorize the release of your PHI. An individual designated as your HIPAA personal representative can also authorize the release of your PHI, but this authorization is governed by specific requirements. In order for the person you designate as your agent to have access to your medical records, the following requirements must be met:

❖   **Writing.** The authorization should be in writing. It should expressly state that your consent is voluntary and that your treatment, payment, and health plan eligibility should not be affected whether or not you authorize the release of information.

❖   **What.** The authorization should describe the health information to be disclosed, whether such information includes your entire medical record or only specified components of that record. You might specify that only those medical records pertaining to certain dates or time periods be released. If you wish alcohol and drug treatment, HIV testing, and mental health information released (or not released), expressly state so. The HIPAA paradigm is that only as much information should be disclosed as necessary. However, it is unreasonable to expect a medical provider to determine what constitutes "necessary" or "unnecessary" for every patient, so the authorization you sign should be explicit.

❖   **Who.** Which medical provider should make the disclosure? This could be a specific neurologist, psychologist, physician, or hospital. Alternatively, it could be a list of several medical care providers or a category of providers. For example, "any physicians, hospitals, or other medical providers who have provided treatment, other medical services or payment for same, from June 1, 2004, through and including the date of this Authorization." How broad or narrow you make the list depends on what your goal is and who you are naming as your agent.

❖   **Term.** When does the authorization to disclose PHI expire? This could be "upon a child attaining age twenty-one," which might suffice for a minor's care. It could be "two years from the signing of the authorization," which should be more than adequate for a life insurance application. "Upon the conclusion of my court case" may suffice for a litigation matter, although issues of appeals, etc., might dictate the parameters to be set. "One year from death" might be used in a health care proxy to ensure your agent has access to your records while you are alive as well as for evaluation of post-death records without the need to qualify as the executor of your estate. If your chronic illness will impact your competency or eventually result in your being incapacitated, you might want to expressly provide that the grant of authority will not lapse. If the authorization involves a trustee, it might be "so long as serving as trustee of the [identify trust]."

❖   **Revocation.** A revocation is a statement that you retain the right to revoke any authorization to disclose your PHI. Any revocation, however, is not binding on a medical provider until received. This minimizes the extent of a provider's liability for disclosing information based on an authorization held prior to the revocation. Obviously, if you are suffering from dementia or other cognitive impairment, at some point you might lack the capacity to revoke the authorization.

❖   **Redisclosure.** The release may state that certain information, such as HIV testing results, cannot be disclosed by the person receiving it. However, the release should also acknowledge that once other information is disclosed, it may thereafter be redisclosed by the person receiving it without violating the HIPAA safeguards.

❖   **Purpose.** The purpose for the disclosure should be explained. This might be limited to the minimum information to determine whether you have the ability to function as a trustee or should be replaced, or only the information necessary to underwrite you for life insurance. However, it is quite likely that you will wish to grant a trusted friend or family member the right to monitor your care throughout your illness, so a broad authorization may be more appropriate in that instance.

❖   **Signer.** If you are signing the authorization, the signature line should merely state that you are the patient. If, however, another person is signing for your (e.g., if your hand coordination prevents you from signing or you have already declined to the point of lacking legal capacity to execute the document), the authorization should state that signatory qualifies as your personal representative under HIPAA, that he or she has authority to make health care decisions for you, and a brief note defining the scope of the representative's authority. It might also be advisable to indicate the source of this person's authority to be your personal representative. For an adult or emancipated minor, this could be a health care proxy, court appointment as guardian, or an agent under your general power of attorney. Arguably, it could be a trustee under a trust agreement, depending on the terms of the trust. For a minor patient, it might be the signer's position as parent or guardian. For an estate, it would most likely be the signer's role as executor.

MENTAL HEALTH INFORMATION

Psychotherapy notes are not required to be released. So don't worry Tony, Dr. Jennifer Melfi's notes are off limits (even if you asked her out while separated from Carmela)!

EMPOWERING AN AGENT TO RELEASE YOUR PHI

There are myriad reasons you might want to have an agent or personal representative act on your behalf with regard to HIPAA matters. This agent can act with the same authority as if he or she were standing in your shoes, but this person must be chosen with care and with a full understanding of legal requirements that must be met when selecting this person. Here's what the law says: "In general, the scope of the personal representative's authority to act for the individual under the Privacy Rule derives from his or her authority under applicable law to make health care decisions for the individual."

The definition is quite nettlesome. If a person has broad authority to make health care decisions for another person, such as a parent for a minor child or a legal guardian for an incompetent adult, that person should generally be treated as stepping into the shoes of the minor or ward for HIPAA purposes. Exceptions may apply in instances of abuse or if state law provides to the contrary. "Where the authority to act for the individual is limited, or specific to particular health care decisions, the personal representative is to be treated as the individual only with respect to protected health information that is relevant to the representation."

Can your agent under your power of attorney be your personal representative? Not necessarily. Your agent under your financial power of attorney is generally not empowered to make health care related decisions. Although paying medical bills may constitute making decisions related to health care, it may not be enough because this person's ability to obtain PHI will be limited to those matters pertaining to paying medical bills. How broad of a medical decision making authority should an agent under your power of attorney be granted? And at what point might your financial agent's authority conflict with your health care agent's? For example, if your financial agent is to make the financial decisions as to which health care facility to pay for, will the agent be entitled to all of the information required to make that decision? In most cases, you probably won't want your financial agent to dictate health care decisions by controlling the payment of matters that should remain within the purview of your health care agent. So you don't want to inadvertently make the HIPAA and related language in your financial power so broad that you undermine the goal of having a separate health care agent make health related decisions.

FIDUCIARIES

The term "fiduciary" means people in a position of trust. This includes agents under your power of attorney and health proxy, as well as your trustee (the person who manages a trust you set up) and your executor (the person who manages your estate when you die). After your death, it is the executor of your estate who automatically becomes your HIPAA personal representative and has the authority to act on your behalf concerning any protected health information.

If you set up a revocable living trust to protect yourself, your trustee and successor trustees will need access to your medical records to pay medical bills and handle other administrative matters. If the same people are also named as agents under your health care proxy to make health care decisions, there should be no problem in doing so. If they are not (which is common, the people named as trustees are usually selected for their business and investment acumen) then the same issues and steps discussed in the preceding section as to how your agent under your power of attorney would deal with HIPAA would apply to your trustees as well.

Chapter Summary

HIPAA affects a broad range of personal, financial, health care, and estate planning transactions. Almost every key estate document, and many important business documents, need to address HIPAA disclosure issues to ensure that various mechanisms (succession of fiduciaries, determinations of disability, etc.) can be triggered. The issues are quite complex but are an important part of planning for your care and future.

HIPAA AUTHORIZATION AND RELEASE FORM

I, *CLIENT NAME (Social Security Number: *SOCIAL SEC #), residing at *CLIENT ADDRESS, being of the age of majority under the laws of *STATE NAME, do hereby declare as follows:

1. Appointment of Agent. I hereby make, constitute, and appoint ("Grant") *AGENT 1 NAME, residing at or doing business at *AGENT 1 ADDRESS to be my agent under the Health Insurance Portability and Accountability Act of 1996, 42 USC 130d and 45 CFR 160-164, and in particular its 2003 Privacy Regulations ("HIPAA") ("Agent").

2. Powers of Agent.

i. My agent shall be treated as I would with regard to the use and dissemination of my individually identifiable health information and medical records.

ii. This authority applies to any information governed by the HIPAA rules and regulations. I specifically authorize any health plan, physician, dentist, health care professional, hospital, clinic, laboratory, pharmacy, medical facility, insurance company and the Medical Information Bureau Inc., or any other health care organization that has provided payment, treatment or services to me or on my behalf or that has paid for or is seeking payment from me for such services (my "Provider") to give, disclose and release to my Agent all of my individually identifiable health information and medical records regarding any past, present or future medical matter, including but not limited to records as to my mental health condition including but not limited to all information relating to the diagnosis and treatment of mental illness and the use of alcohol or drugs. This authorization specifically includes psychotherapy notes. "Psychotherapy notes" means notes recorded (in any medium) by a health care provider who is a mental health professional documenting or analyzing the contents of conversation during a private counseling session or a group, joint, or family counseling session and that are separate from the rest of my medical records.

iii. I specifically authorize the release of medication prescription and monitoring, counseling session start and stop times, the modalities and frequencies of treatment furnished, results of clinical tests, and any summary of the following items: diagnosis, functional status, the treatment plan, symptoms, prognosis, and progress to date.

iv. The purpose of this Release is to address my current and future care in light of the current and potential future impact of my chronic illness, I have expressly made this grant of authority to the agents listed broad in terms of Protected Health Information they can access, the medical providers including covered entities that should disclose information to my agent, and the duration of this authorization. I expressly intend that this grant continue in such broad capacity if I shall in the future be incapacitated.

v. This Authorization is expressly made valid for all documents held by any medical providers including any covered entity that has or shall hereafter provided me with medical or related or ancillary care.

3. Prior Agreements with Providers. The authority given to my Agent by this Authorization shall supersede any prior agreement I have made to restrict my personal health information and unless specifically noted, and I instruct my Providers to release and disclose to my Agent my entire medical record without restriction as set forth in this Authorization.

4. Indemnification. All persons and entities shall not incur any liability to me or my estate as a result of permitting my Agent access to any information or to exercise any power relating to my medical condition. I hereby agree to indemnify and hold harmless any such third party from and against any and all claims that may arise against such third party by reason of such third party having relied on the provisions of this instrument.

5. Copies of Document. A copy, facsimile, and PDF of this Authorization are as valid as the original.

6. Competency to Execute Document.   I understand the full import of this document and I am emotionally and mentally competent to execute it.

7. Disability Does Not Affect Validity of this Document. This Authorization shall not, to the extent permitted by applicable law, be affected by my disability as principal, and I do hereby so provide, it being my intention that all powers conferred upon my Agent herein or any substitute designated by me shall remain at all times in full force and effect, notwithstanding my incapacity, disability, or any uncertainty with regard thereto. This provision shall be interpreted in the broadest terms so as to remain in effect throughout my disability to the fullest extent provided for under the laws of state in which it is executed. Because I presently have a chronic illness for which there is no known cure, I recognize that the grant of authority hereunder will be for the duration of my lifetime. I understand and expressly reaffirm the broad time horizon for this document.

8. Construction and Interpretation of this Document. This instrument is to be construed and interpreted as a HIPAA release authorization for medical, health care and related matters. The enumeration of specific items, rights, acts or powers herein is not intended to, nor does it limit or restrict, and is not to be construed or interpreted as limiting or restricting the general powers herein granted to said Agent. This instrument is executed and delivered in the state indicated below, and the laws of the state of shall govern all questions as to the validity of this power and the construction of its provisions. Should any provisions or power in this document not be enforceable, such enforceability shall not affect the enforceability of the rest of this document. Should this grant be prohibited by any law presently existing or hereinafter enacted, it is my specific desire that such grant be interpreted in the broadest manner permitted by such law, and that in the event such grant is prohibited, that every other provision of this Authorization shall remain fully valid and enforceable.

9. Effective Date. This Authorization shall be effective as of the date it is executed.

10. No Time Limit; Duration.

a. I have considered the possibility of limiting the effectiveness of this instrument to a fixed period of time from the date hereof but have intentionally chosen not to do so.

b. I have decided that it shall remain in full force and effect for as long as I may live unless terminated as provided below.

c. Unless this Authorization is revoked in writing by me, with actual delivery of said revocation to the person or entity in question, it shall continue to be in force and effect and shall expressly not expire.

11. Revocation. I understand that a revocation is not effective to the extent that any of my Providers have relied on this.

12. Redisclosure. I understand that any information that is disclosed pursuant to this authorization may be re-disclosed and no longer covered by federal rules governing privacy and confidentiality of health information.

13. Termination.
a. This Authorization shall be modified or terminated, as the case may be, upon my executing a termination document or upon my executing a written notice of modification or termination and such Agent's receipt of same. I recognize that should I lack the competency to revoke this Authorization, at that future point in time this Authorization will not be able to be revoked. I expressly intend this result and request that any medical provider respect this wish.

b. As to any Provider, this Authorization shall be modified or terminated, as the case may be, upon such Provider receiving actual notice of a modification or termination.

IN WITNESS WHEREOF, I have hereunto set my hand and seal this *MONTH *DAY, *YEAR.

_____

*CLIENT NAME

Witness: _____

State of *STATE-EXECUTION

County of *COUNTY NAME

　　　BE IT REMEMBERED, that on this *MONTH *DAY, *YEAR, before me, the subscriber, a notary of the State of *STATE-EXECUTION, personally appeared *CLIENT NAME who, I am satisfied after inspection of *STATE NAME #driver's license, is the principal mention in, and who executed the above HIPAA Authorization and Release and acknowledged that he or she signed, sealed and delivered the same as his or her act and deed, that he or she appeared to be of sound mind and not under any duress, fraud or undue influence, and for the uses and purposes therein expressed.

_____

Notary Signature

CHAPTER 7

Your Health Care Proxy and Living Will

Designating Someone to Make Health Care Decisions for You

Introduction to Health Care Proxies and Living Wills

A HEALTH CARE PROXY IS A LEGAL DOCUMENT in which you designate a trusted person (agent) to make health care decisions for you if you are unable to do so yourself because of illness or disability. A living will is a statement that defines your health care wishes. Although the two documents are integrally related, having them prepared and executed as independent documents may facilitate their use in many instances. Some health care providers prefer a health care proxy so that they can have your named agent execute documents confirming health care decisions. In other situations, hospitals or medical facilities may insist on a living will simply because of their policies. In many instances, a detailed personalized explanation of your health care wishes, as provided by a living will, may be essential to provide guidance to those making decisions for you.

The focus of the health care proxy is for you to appoint someone as your agent to make health care decisions. Some states do not afford the same recognition to a living will as they do to a health care proxy. In those states, the health care proxy empowering your agent will be the only document with legal weight. Nevertheless, the personal details in your living will remain an important source of insight into your wishes. No matter which document you use to indicate your health care decisions, it should be prepared in a manner that presents "clear and convincing" proof of your wishes. Vague and general statements as to "no heroic measures" and the like, which are typically used in many boilerplate living wills may not suffice. Therefore, the safest approach is for you to sign both a living will and a health care proxy, making certain that your wishes are clearly and convincingly stated, and have each of the documents witnessed and notarized separately. To be "clear and convincing" will often require you to elaborate on the standard language many forms contain. This is especially important in light of the impact of your health status. You should really endeavor to custom tailor the statements in your living will and health care proxy so that they clearly show how your chronic illness impacts your directives.

The health care proxy (power of attorney for medical directives) provides a mechanism for decisions to be made by your chosen representatives if, when, and where the need exists. It is impossible to foresee every possible future illness or every possible treatment your doctors may prescribe no matter how "clear and convincing" you try to make the language in your document. By appointing a person to act in your behalf, you ensure that these decisions can be made based on your condition at a given time and that the decisions about available medical procedures and recommendations are made in accordance with your wishes.

EXAMPLE

You might have a very specific view of pain relief and how this relates to your illness. You may also have views on "heroic medical efforts" or hospice care that differ (modestly or substantially) from the standard language and explanations that most attorneys normally use to define them. Most people signing these documents have no idea what, if any, health issues may affect them in the future, and this is why most forms are so generic. For people with chronic illnesses, the paradigm is different. You likely have significant knowledge of your current condition and most likely have a pretty good idea about likely future health issues. Use this knowledge to tailor standard forms. Don't accept generic language that really doesn't address your concerns. It is also important to make room for hope in your documents. There is fascinating, cutting-edge research being conducted that may well result in a breakthrough for your particular illness. In the event a significant breakthrough occurs, it is important for your agent to have the flexibility to react and change decisions made before the breakthrough.

IMPORTANCE OF YOUR LIVING WILL

A living will is one of the most important and personal documents that you will ever sign. It is also one of the most controversial, misunderstood, and misapplied legal documents. As with too many important decisions, living wills have become a "quick fix" that seldom address everything that should be addressed. Here are some of the mistakes that people make with living wills:

❖ Sign a quick one-page standard form with your lawyer and your worries are over. Unfortunately, important legal, financial, religious, and medical issues will not be addressed unless you are proactive.

❖ An even worse approach is to use a form you purchase on the internet. Most of these forms are so generic and so poorly drafted that extreme caution is in order.

❖ The worst approach of all is to sign a form a hospital employee hands you when you are admitted because you've taken no action in advance. Regardless of the quality of a hospital provided form, signing a document during the chaos and stress of an emergency hospital admission is never wise.

The information provided below will guide you through the process of properly communicating your wishes. It will explain how you can obtain the best protection and comfort from your living will and health care proxy in a simple and practical manner. It will also give you ideas how to tailor these documents to reflect some of the unique issues created by your special situation. There are various methods of communicating your wishes to the attorney you are working with, and this process should begin with identifying questions or concerns you may have. With this attention to detail, your attorney can more thoroughly and economically assist you in the preparation of a comprehensive living will and health care proxy. Once this process is completed, the final forms will help you inform and guide your family, loved ones, and health care providers in making many vital medical decisions. Your documents should minimize the legal interference and complications of carrying out your wishes.

WHY YOU NEED A LIVING WILL AND HEALTH CARE PROXY

Deciding how you should be cared for in the event of a medical crisis related to your chronic illness, the deterioration of your condition, or even an unrelated medical event, is extraordinarily difficult and emotional. The importance of making your wishes about health care treatment known in the event you are unable to communicate your decisions when you are gravely ill has become an integral part of estate and personal planning for everyone. Without advance preparation, living wills and health care proxies (the documents used to communicate your health care wishes), your health care wishes may not be carried out. Without proper documentation, your family or loved ones may face gut-wrenching decisions about your care. There is no solace to be found in knowing what you would have wanted and not being able to act (or not act) on that knowledge.

In some cases, family members and loved ones do not know what you want, and this makes decision making even more difficult. Thinking about and discussing terminal illness and death can never be a pleasant or easy matter. However, your failure to provide your loved ones with guidance now, while you are able to, may cause them to have to second-guess what you would have wanted done. This will be a far more difficult and emotionally traumatic task for them.

It is thus essential to communicate guidelines, in writing, about how you want to be cared for in the event of a medical emergency, deterioration of your condition (whether anticipated or unexpected), or your terminal illness. They must have the legal authority to do so. Not completing this admittedly unpleasant process now can only create more costs, difficulties, and unpleasantness later—for you and your loved ones. Your personal goals will be compromised and you may spend the final months or years of your life in agony or confronting quality-of-life issues that are unacceptable.

If you do not address living will and related health care issues now, you leave yourself open to having doctors, courts, or others making decisions for you, often with results that you would not have chosen. Remember you have a distinct advantage over those people who do not know what lies ahead because your knowledge about your current illness and the course it may take can help you make choices about many of the medical issues that will affect you in the future.

Why A Comprehensive Document Is Important

The kind of document recommended in this discussion is more comprehensive than what is provided in many of the commercial forms you can purchase in office supply stores or obtain from various organizations. Often the commercial forms are limited to simple instructions such as "pulling the plug" in the event of a terminal illness. This language can be particularly dangerous. Your chronic illness may be "terminal," but you may have a nearly normal life expectancy of many decades. The simplistic language in many standard forms might effectively imply that you don't want any medical intervention, even in the present, hopefully something that does not conform with your wishes in the least. Consider ALS disease, for example, which might be viewed as "terminal" in the sense that it will shorten your life. However, some people with ALS have survived for decades. Directives on a standard form might imply no further care or intervention should be provided. If you want protection against this kind of ambiguity and lack of precision, you need a much more comprehensive document.

The form you use must address your personal needs and concerns, not simply a generic list of choices. Your personal preferences, religious concerns, family, and other personal relationships should all be considered.

Choosing Your Health Care Agent

Choosing whom to appoint as your agent can be very difficult. Many loved ones, however sensitive to your feelings, may simply not be able to make the very difficult decisions that might become necessary as your health deteriorates. Sadly, many people living with chronic illness discover that close family, rather than circling the wagons in support, head for the hills. This, obviously, limits your choices considerably and also suggests that you may have to think about appointing someone who is not part of your immediate family.

Another point that must be made here is that you should never name two or more people to make a joint decision. There are two important reasons for this, the most obvious being that making decisions in a crisis is difficult enough without having to make a decision with someone who may disagree with you. Furthermore, some state laws prohibit joint agents, which will make the appointment ineffectual. If you want to name two people to make decisions, name them sequentially (that is, the second only can serve if the first cannot). You can then add nonbinding language to the health care proxy suggesting, but not requiring, that all agents consult each other (if feasible) before acting. This recommendation might, in fact, be made in a separate letter of instruction, a tactic that allows you to express your wishes without inviting unnecessary legal issues.

Do not necessarily assume that the person you select will be able to carry out your wishes. Some prospective agents may have religious, moral, or other personal reasons for not being willing to carry out certain wishes. For example, many people simply do not have the emotional composition to "pull the plug." You should discuss these important matters with every potential agent or successor agent in advance. You should also request permission from the people you want to name as your agent or successor agent; the person appointed should not discover he has been appointed via a phone call from some hospital in the middle of the night.

Be very careful in naming a child to make your health care decisions. Many children, even those who have long ago reached the age of majority, have a very difficult time making tough medical decisions for a parent, especially an end-of-life decision. If you want to name children, find out in advance whether they are comfortable with accepting this responsibility and the choices it might entail. If you have more than one child, in what order do you name them? (Remember that some states prohibit joint agents and that appointing joint agents may create conflicts between the individuals appointed). Do you name them in age order? What if your middle child is a physician or nurse, do you name that child first and then the remaining children in age order? Furthermore, you should recognize that requiring more than one signature for documents related to your treatment might guarantee that the required decisions will not be made in time.

Consider your state's health care statutes for any requirements that they may impose on health care agents. Your attorney can advise you about this, or you can review the statute books at your local library or online. Find a web site (preferably an official state web site) that covers state laws and research your state's policies on living wills, health care agents, or similar subjects.

ADDITIONAL DECISIONS YOU SHOULD MAKE

There are a host of significant personal decisions you must make to best protect your wishes. These decisions should reflect any nuances of your current and anticipated health status. The paragraphs below provide examples of common issues that affect decisions made by people with chronic illnesses.

NO HEROIC MEASURES OR ALL MEASURES

Should mechanical means of prolonging your life be used? One difficulty in addressing this question is that it is impossible to know which treatments will be necessary or available. Furthermore, how do you define "heroic"? What is heroic in one situation may not be heroic in another. If you have ALS, you will assuredly need assistance breathing at some point, and standard forms mandating intubation or no intubation may not be precise enough to reflect your wishes. On the other hand, some forms get quite specific, giving you a complex grid of boxes to check off the types of medical procedures you want or don't want, based on various hypothetical scenarios. But what happens if your scenario is just a little different from what's in the boxes? What should your agent do then? In some cases, having too many choices is worse than having none. In other cases, not even a form that covers hundreds or thousands of options and potential scenarios can get it right—there is simply no guarantee that it will address the unique nuances of your chronic illness or some unanticipated turn of events. Consider different options and provisions and make the choices that are best for you. Review these choices with your health care provider; your doctors and others may help you refine your decisions. If your religion is an important part of your life, you may want to consult with clergy as well.

With so much press and attention given to the right to die, euthanasia, cessation of medical procedures, and related issues, one very important fact has been obscured. Many people want every medically reasonable method, heroic or not, performed, and you may be one of the many. If, for example, there is a breakthrough medical development in the wings that may have a dramatic impact on your chronic illness, you may want every measure taken so that you are still around if and when the breakthrough materializes. You may be more than willing to pursue experimental and new procedures if they can potentially reverse your illness. Most standardized forms don't even address this because they tend to reflect the current broad tendency to prohibit heroic measures. If you do want every life-saving procedure and extraordinary measures (cardiac resuscitation, mechanical respiration, nutrition, hydration) performed, your living will should state this. If you want this only if there is a new potential treatment for your disease, then tailor the language to reflect this.

EXAMPLE • *Alzheimer's Disease*

The certainty of cognitive impairment affects end-of-life decisions and suggests modification of standard language and forms for those living with AD. Language in a living will should be tailored to reflect the specific realities of AD. It should also be tailored to address other potential illnesses: If you have AD, you may eventually succumb to other illnesses (stroke, pneumonia, etc.), not AD.

Sample Standard Provision

"If I have an incurable or irreversible, severe mental or severe physical condition; or am in a state of permanent unconsciousness or profound dementia; or am severely injured; or if I have a terminal illness, as defined below, then no heroic measures shall be performed. For purposes of the above, "terminal illness" shall be defined as an irreversible, incurable, and untreatable condition caused by disease, illness, or injury when an attending physician can certify in writing that, to a reasonable degree of medical certainty, there is no hope of my recovery or death is likely to occur in a brief period of time if life-sustaining treatment is not provided. In these situations I wish that no heroic measures be taken to preserve or prolong my life . . . "

Below, this provision has been revised to reflect the reality of AD.

Sample Alzheimer's Disease Modified Provision

"I have Alzheimer's disease, which is incurable and irreversible and which will result in dementia. Therefore, when I reach a stage of profound Alzheimer's disease when I have a nearly complete or a complete lack of awareness of my surroundings, I wish that no heroic measures be taken to preserve my life. If I reach a stage of severe

Alzheimer's marked by disorientation psychosis, delusions, paranoia, and/or hallucinations, and also am severely injured, or have a terminal illness (for purposes of the above, "terminal illness" shall be defined as an irreversible, incurable, and untreatable condition caused by disease, illness, or injury when an attending physician can certify in writing that, to a reasonable degree of medical certainty, there is no hope of my recovery or death is likely to occur in a brief period of time, defined as 90 days, if life-sustaining treatment is not provided), then I wish that no heroic measures be taken to preserve my life. Further, if I am then in a state of severe dementia, the 90-day period above should be extended to one year. Notwithstanding the forgoing, if a new treatment is available that could potentially reverse my AD and potentially restore some reasonable quality of life and cognitive ability such that I could conceivably communicate with my loved ones, then all heroic measures shall be taken, including but not limited to the provision of the new or experimental therapy. In no event shall any Agent or medical provider making this decision be held liable for their interpretation of this provision."

NUTRITION AND HYDRATION

You should specifically state whether you would permit your agent to ever withdraw artificial nutrition and hydration. If you do not wish to have artificial feeding, even if discontinuing it could hasten your death, this should be specifically stated. Many states will not permit the cessation of nutrition or hydration unless the patient's living will specifically authorizes it. Because some states require a separate signature (next to the provision) in any health care proxy that permits an agent to withdraw nutrition or hydration, it may be a good idea to sign this provision just to make sure your wishes are not ignored because of a technicality.

Several additional issues can create confusion. How, for example, should "artificial" be defined? Should a distinction be made between withdrawing nutrition and hydration (e.g., a feeding tube) and withholding the initial connection to artificial feeding tubes? Do your religious beliefs affect this decision? The core beliefs of many religions equate the withdrawal, and in some cases the withholding (or nonprovision), of nutrition and hydration as the equivalent of starving someone to death. For this reason, you must consider the religious sensitivities of the people you designate as your health care agents. If someone you want to name agent would have to violate his or her fundamental religious beliefs to carry out your wishes, deal with this issue now. Depending on your relationship with this individual and your own religious or moral convictions, you may decide to modify your wishes, name a different agent, or get clarification from a religious authority before finalizing your decision.

QUALITY-OF-LIFE STATEMENTS

Your living will may be the only written evidence of what your deepest personal wishes are. Therefore, it should as clearly and as precisely as possible state your feelings and wishes about health care, treatment, quality of life, whether you may wish to refuse or accept medical treatment, and so forth. The law may require that the living will demonstrate your intent with "clear and convincing evidence." This applies in particularly significant ways to quality-of-life issues. Many living wills contain general language stating that if there is "no quality of life," then "no heroic measures" should be taken to prolong life. But "no quality of life" means different things to different people. For one person, it might mean the inability to communicate to the outside world, with no anticipation of recovery. For someone else, it might mean severe and ongoing pain that cannot be alleviated. Chronic illnesses are, by definition, long-term illnesses, so that you have some understanding of what your future holds. Make specific quality-of-life decisions that work for you. For a young athletic person whose biggest health issue has been a hangnail, the thought of being confined to a wheelchair may appear so traumatic that he or she might in fact define that as "no quality of life" and decline all heroic measures. (Note that such people often change their minds about this, preferring to fight than succumb without trying.) Someone who has lived with multiple sclerosis with minimal effect and has recently been told that a motorized scooter will replace walking as a result of the progression of the MS, may react differently. While not a choice this person might have made voluntarily, it may be a choice that can be lived with, particularly as it permits the individual to engage in normal activities, albeit in a different mode. For you, the definition of quality of life will differ from that presented in either of these examples. It is, in every case, a personal decision that reflects not only physical and mental change but also personal beliefs and numerous other factors that define who you are. Analyze your own feelings and concerns about quality of life and make your wishes explicit.

GUARDIAN DESIGNATION

If your illness will (or may) result in your eventual inability to manage your affairs and person to the extent that a guardian must be appointed, consider taking the following two steps. First, address all the planning issues and documents presented in this book, especially focusing on a funded revocable living trust. The second step is to include an express provision in your health proxy naming your health proxy as your guardian. Both steps can prevent the need for a court appointed guardian.

There are, generally speaking, two types of guardians. A guardian of your person makes health and living decisions, and a guardian of your property primarily makes financial decisions. Ideally, you should choose who will be making these decisions on your behalf. At a minimum, you should designate your health care agent as both or at least the guardian of your person. The objective here is to make your wishes known before guardianship becomes an issue. In the event a court in the future has to appoint a guardian, you have made known your wishes about whom that person should be. While there is no guarantee that the court will follow your wishes, significant weight will be given to your designation (especially if your health care proxy is notarized and has two witnesses).

Sample Provision

> "To the extent that I am permitted by law to do so, I hereby nominate my Agent, FINANCIAL AGENT NAME, to serve as the guardian of my property, and my Health Proxy, HEALTH AGENT NAME, to serve as the guardian of my person, or in any similar representative capacity, and if I am not permitted by law to so nominate, then I request that any court that may be involved in the appointment of a guardian, special medical guardian, conservator or similar representative for me give the greatest weight to this request."

ANATOMICAL GIFTS (ORGAN DONATIONS)

Organ donations help save the lives of others, and it is hoped that you will seriously and carefully give thought to donating your organs after your death. If, however, you do not wish to permit organ donation, you should indicate so in your living will.

Many people erroneously assume that organ donations are prohibited for religious reasons. Often they are not. Do not dismiss organ donations for religious reasons alone unless you have consulted your religious adviser. If the idea of donating your organs to strangers is distasteful to you, consider restricting the provision rather than eliminating it altogether. For example, would you refuse to donate an organ or organs that might save the life of someone you love?

If organ donation is something you believe in and support, you might wish to include an express provision concerning donating tissue samples for research to help others with the same chronic illness you have. The language should be specific enough to ensure that the tissues will be used for research or for whatever specific goal you have in mind. Even if you have a general religious preference against organ donations, you may want to make this an exception. If so, then clearly state that although your stated religious preferences should apply to all other decisions, you have expressly excluded the application of those religious strictures to the donation of tissue for research. You can make a great difference with this simple step.

Sample Provision

> "Because I have lived for many decades with multiple sclerosis, I expressly include this provision directing the donation of brain or central nervous system tissue samples for MS research efforts, but for no other purpose. I expressly note and acknowledge that my core religious preferences may mandate against organ donations. Nevertheless, I expressly wish to provide for these tissue donations in spite of any such strictures."

BURIAL INSTRUCTIONS

If you desire any specific eulogy, service, or steps taken, specify your wishes in your living will. If you want a traditional religious ceremony, say so. If you want to be cremated rather than buried, say so. Alternatively, you can communicate these and other desires in a letter of last instructions.

RELIGION

Religious preferences or lack thereof should be specified. For those with strong religious convictions, it is imperative to specifically address religious concerns to avoid having your beliefs compromised when you may be unable to express your desires. Since health care wishes are such a personal matter, it is also vital to address religious concerns to prevent family members or others involved with your health care from pushing their beliefs (or lack of beliefs) on you. For example, if you are Catholic and wish to have last rites, your living will should so state.

The legal community, right-to-die organizations, and many others involved with the health care decision process have all but ignored religious considerations assuming that most people signing living wills while they are healthy aren't concerned about religious issues. These organizations, however, fail to comprehend that many of these same people, when faced with a major catastrophe such as terminal illness or loss of a close family member, fall back on their religious roots for guidance and comfort. Unfortunately, in the case of chronic illnesses that eventually lead to cognitive impairment, it may then be too late for these people or their loved ones to express spiritual changes. The solution is to think about this issue and the religious implications of the entire health care process while you are able to. In the end, there will be no regrets that something important was not addressed. (For more detail on religion and its potential impact on estate planning, see Chapter 12.)

Whether or not you have any religious convictions, your living will should communicate your decisions. If you were born to parents with a particular religious affiliation, other members of your family could assume that it would be appropriate to consult with clergy of your religious background before making a decision. This may or may not be what you wish to have done. Religiously influenced decisions can well be different from what you want. For example, several religions restrict the ability to stop heroic measures. If you want nutrition and hydration withdrawn if there is no hope of your regaining quality of life, it is important to communicate whether you wish religious principles to be considered in making this decision.

Religious doctrines may have a very specific effect on what can be done medically to sustain or not sustain life. However you presently feel about the effects the tenets of your faith may have on these decisions, it can be a terrible mistake not to address these issues with your clergy. Your family's religious convictions should also be considered. With some modification, it may be possible to carry out your wishes in a manner that does not negate the religious tenets of your faith.

If you decide, after consulting with your clergy and discussions with your family, that you wish to take a position contrary to the tenets of your faith (e.g., for tissue donations as discussed above), your living will should indicate this in very precise terms. You may wish to provide the name and address of a clergy member to your attorney so that the clergy member can be consulted for interpretations of your religious beliefs. You should include in a note of instruction, and in some instances even in your legal documents, the name of the religious adviser to be contacted if a decision has to be made concerning your care and the decision cannot be easily made without religious interpretation. Also, you should include the name and contact data for the religious organization or institution to be contacted should the clergy member you named be unavailable. It is quite important that you discuss these matters with your personal religious adviser before you meet with your lawyer.

PAIN RELIEF

What about pain medication and other treatments or procedures to reduce pain? Should they be administered even if they hasten death? Is there any adverse religious implications if pain relief hastens death? Should a distinction be made between the side effects of pain relief somewhat hastening death versus affirmatively using pain medication in doses intended to cause death? How can this distinction be made? Are there any specific implications of your illness that may effect how you want to mandate pain relief? Your answers to these and similar questions should become part of your living will.

WILL AMBULANCE AND EMERGENCY MEDICAL TECHNICIANS ACCEPT A LIVING WILL?

The primary goal of ambulance and emergency medical technicians is saving lives, or more specifically, keeping a patient alive until he or she reaches a hospital. The urgent nature of their activities, the time frame of their involvement, and their primary mission make it difficult if not impossible for them to review, interpret, and then apply the provisions of your living will. Plan in advance.

If you are terminally ill or at a stage of dementia at which you would not want heroic measures, you may prefer to consider alternative transportation arrangements to the hospital to avoid having the emergency personnel performing heroic measures in the ambulance. Discuss this with your health care agents and doctor in advance.

WHAT ABOUT OLD LIVING WILLS?

It is best to locate and destroy old living wills. This is especially wise if your prior living will and health proxy were signed prior to your diagnosis. Being diagnosed with a chronic illness changes almost everything, including how you view any future health care issues. Most likely, your wishes and needs will have evolved significantly and the modifications will be reflected in your new living will. The danger of keeping old living wills is that they may inadvertently surface at the wrong time in the wrong place (or in the wrong hands) and cause unnecessary confusion. To preclude such an event, make sure the appropriate people have the newest living will you have signed. You might also consider including a provision revoking any and all prior living wills. However, it is still best to locate and destroy these prior documents.

WHAT TO DO WITH YOUR SIGNED LIVING WILL FORMS

Give a copy of your living will and health care proxy to your primary care doctor. Give your initial agent, and at least one successor agent, an original. Your attorney will retain a signed original for an emergency. Most importantly, keep an original at home in an accessible location.

OTHER STEPS YOU SHOULD TAKE

DISCUSS YOUR DECISIONS

The process by which you determine what your living will should contain is just as important as the documents you sign. This process should therefore include candid discussions about your feelings with your family, loved ones, doctor, and religious adviser (if applicable). All of these people may be involved in the decisions concerning your health care if you should become unable to express your own wishes. They cannot be expected to carry out your desires without knowing what those desires are and how you feel about them. The more openly you discuss your feelings with family, friends, and loved ones, the more likely that you can ease the burden of decision making they face. While your religious adviser can assist your doctors and family in reaching a decision that is in accordance with applicable religious tenets and your personal beliefs, an awareness of your feelings can be important in properly guiding your family and physicians. The process of communicating your beliefs and feelings is very important steps; it cannot be accomplished by signing a quick-fix form with your lawyer.

COORDINATE YOUR HEALTH CARE AND FINANCIAL DOCUMENTS

A durable power of attorney with financial powers is an integral part of your health care (and estate) planning. If the agent you authorize does not have the financial wherewithal, or the legal access to your funds to carry out your health care wishes, then your desires could also be stymied. Financial considerations should be addressed as a separate document since some states do not permit the grant of health care and financial powers in the same document. This can be particularly important if your attitude about the religious implications of a living will or health care proxy differs from that of family members. As an alternative, a living trust (not to be confused with a living will), which is also called a revocable inter vivos trust, can be used. When properly prepared, this document can address a broad range of financial and other issues, including the handling of your financial matters in the event of disability, much more comprehensively than a power of attorney. The living trust remains a powerful and flexible financial planning tool for handling your financial matters in the event of disability. To make your power of attorney or living trust effective, be certain that your attorney-in-fact or trustees have adequate financial information to locate and marshal your assets for your benefit. The best legal documents are useless if family members can't locate your bank or securities accounts to apply your assets to meet your health care wishes.

CARRY A POCKET CARD

Whatever your wishes concerning your health care, properly prepared documents are far too bulky to carry on your person. In an emergency situation, your attending physicians can at least be informed by a wallet card that you signed a living will and health care proxy, and whom to contact. It might also specify the major health issues you face. This is especially important if you don't wear a medical identification bracelet or other identifying device.

CONSIDER THE POLICIES OF A PARTICULAR HEALTH CARE FACILITY

If you are going to enter a nursing home or other health care facility, be certain to review its policies about fundamental health care issues. If the organization's policies are incompatible with your health care wishes, you may wish to evaluate alternative facilities. For example, if the facility is sponsored by a Catholic organization, there may be a strict policy against assisted suicide or euthanasia. This policy may not be affected no matter what is stated in your living will. A Jewish health care facility may have a policy of administering nutrition and hydration unless medically contraindicated. If you are a Jehovah's Witness, identify medical institutions familiar with and able to address your special religious/medical needs. In some cases, if you have chosen a particular course of action in your living will, you may need to select the medical facility with similar policies about care and advance planning.

CHAPTER SUMMARY

This chapter has reviewed two key health care decision documents: your living will and health care proxy. These documents are important to your dignity as a human being, to minimize emotional stress on your loved ones, and to ensure that your wishes are respected. This means taking the time and effort to craft these documents to address any current known health conditions, the likely issues that may arise in the future as a result of your chronic illness, and any religious convictions you have.

LIVING WILL

I, *YOUR NAME, residing at *YOUR ADDRESS, being an adult and of sound mind, and being competent and otherwise capable of making the decisions set forth in this Living Will, and having the fundamental right to make voluntary, informed choices to accept, reject, or choose among alternative courses of medical and surgical treatment, make this declaration as a directive to be followed if for any reason I become unable to participate in decisions regarding my medical care, this statement shall stand as an expression of my wishes, beliefs, objectives and directions (my "Wishes"). It is my specific intent that my Wishes, as stated herein constitute clear and convincing evidence of such Wishes.

1. Recitals.

a. **WHEREFORE**, I direct that this Living Will become a part of my permanent medical records. I expressly authorize any medical care provider to rely on the statements in this Living Will if it is not feasible in an emergency situation to reach my Health Care Agent. This Living Will shall serve as general guidance for my Agent appointed under my separate Health Care Proxy or Health Care Power of Attorney. However, in all circumstances, medical care providers may defer to the judgment and interpretation of my Health Care Agent of the terms of this Living Will and shall in no event be held liable for relying on my Health Care Agent's interpretations. I expressly recognize that it is impossible to conceive of all situations that may occur in a living will so that my Agent may address all such circumstances using the guidelines contained in this Living Will.

b. **WHEREFORE**, I wish to direct the actions of my family, friends, physicians, nurses, and all those concerned with my care, as provided in this declaration.

c. **WHEREFORE**, I hereby express my hope that my Wishes be honored by health care facilities and physicians without having to go through the process of any judicial or other determination.

NOW THEREFORE, I declare my wishes to be as follows:

2. Current, Known, or Suspected Medical Conditions.

a. *Comment*: *Describe any current medical conditions and how it may impact medical decision making.*

3. No Heroic Medical Efforts.

a. General 'No Heroic Measures' Language.

(1) *Comment: Chronic Illness: You may want every medically reasonable method, heroic or not, performed. If there is a breakthrough medical development in the wings that may have a dramatic impact on your chronic illness, you may want every measure taken. You may be more than willing to pursue experimental and new procedures if they could potentially reverse your illness. Most standardized forms not only don't contemplate this, but would likely result in treating these as prohibited "heroic measures." If you want every life-saving procedure and extraordinary measures (cardiac resuscitation, mechanical respiration, nutrition, hydration) performed, your living will should state this. If you only want this if there is a new potential treatment for your disease, then tailor the language to reflect this. The illustrative provision below for someone with Alzheimer's disease can provide guidance as to how you can modify the general provisions later to reflect your personal situation.*

(2) ***Sample Alzheimer's Disease Provision to Modify for Various Health Issues:*** "I have Alzheimer's disease which is incurable and irreversible and which will result in dementia. Therefore, when I reach a stage of profound Alzheimer's disease and I have a nearly complete or a complete lack of awareness of my surroundings, I wish that no heroic measures be taken to preserve my life. If I reach a stage of severe Alzheimer's marked by disorientation psychosis, delusions, paranoia, and/or hallucinations, and also am severely injured, or have a terminal illness (For purposes of the above, "terminal illness" shall be defined as an irreversible, incurable, and untreatable condition caused by disease, illness, or injury when an attending physician

can certify in writing that, to a reasonable degree of medical certainty, there is no hope of my recovery or death is likely to occur in a brief period of time, defined as 90 days, if life-sustaining treatment is not provided) then I wish that no heroic measures be taken to preserve my life. Further, if I am then in a state of severe dementia the 90-day period above should be extended to one year. Notwithstanding the forgoing, if a new treatment is available that could potentially reverse my AD and potentially restore some reasonable quality of life and cognitive ability such that I could conceivably communicate with my loved ones, then all heroic measures shall be taken including but not limited to the provision of the new or experimental therapy. In no event shall any Agent or medical provider making this decision be held liable for their interpretation of this provision."

(3) ***General No Heroic Measures Language.*** If:

(a) I have an incurable or irreversible, severe mental or severe physical condition; or am in a state of permanent unconsciousness or profound dementia; or am severely injured, or have a terminal illness (for purposes of the above, "terminal illness" shall be defined as an irreversible, incurable, and untreatable condition caused by disease, illness, or injury when an attending physician can certify in writing that, to a reasonable degree of medical certainty, there is no hope of my recovery or death is likely to occur in a brief period of time if life-sustaining treatment is not provided. "Permanently unconscious" is defined as a state that, to a reasonable degree of medical certainty, an attending physician certifies in writing that I am irreversibly unaware of myself and my environment and there is a total loss of cerebral cortical functioning resulting in my having no capacity to experience pain); and

(b) In any of these cases there is no reasonable expectation of recovering from such severe, permanent condition, and regaining any meaningful quality of life, then in any such event, it is my desire and intent that heroic life-sustaining procedures and extraordinary maintenance or medical treatment be withheld and withdrawn.

(c) Quality of life is of tremendous importance in determining the scope and extent of health care services which I wish to receive. Maintaining my life as a mere biological existence, in a vegetative state, is not an acceptable goal of my medical treatment. Therefore, if there is no reasonable probability (i.e., negligible probability) that any particular medical treatment would benefit me by returning me to a level of functioning or existence where I could communicate with my loved ones, and reasonably understand such communication, I direct that medical treatments, as described herein, be withheld and withdrawn.

(1) ***Comment:*** *Should the "quality of life" provisions be modified? Many living wills contain general statements that if there is "no quality of life," then "no heroic measures" should be taken to prolong your life. No quality of life might mean to one person the inability to communicate to the outside world, with no anticipation of recovery. To another person no quality of life may mean severe and ongoing pain that cannot be abated. Chronic illnesses by definition are long term so that you have some understanding of what your future holds. Make specific decisions that work for you. For a young athletic person whose biggest health issue has been a hangnail, the thought of being confined to a wheel chair may appear so traumatic that they might in fact define that as insufficient quality of life and believe that they would decline heroic measures (such people often revise their feelings on this as life deals them greater doses of reality). The fact that you may require a motorized scooter as a result of the progression of your Multiple Sclerosis, while not a choice you would have voluntarily made, may have had little impact on your personal and business activities. For you, the definition of quality of life will differ from that of the young person above.*

(d) It is not my desire to prolong my life through mechanical means where my body is no longer able to perform vital bodily functions on its own, and where there is little likelihood of ever regaining any meaningful quality of life. The condition and degree of severity and permanence contemplated by this provision are of such a nature and degree of permanent illness, injury, disability, or accompanied by pain such that the average person would make the decisions I have made herein.

(e) In any such event, I direct all physicians and medical facilities in whose care I may be, and my family and all those concerned with my care, to refrain from and cease extraordinary or heroic life sustaining treatment to be withheld and withdrawn (i.e., to be considered heroic) include, without limitation, surgery, antibiotics, cardiac and pulmonary resuscitation, ventilation, intubation, or other respiratory support (except as provided otherwise under the provision below 'Nutrition and Hydration'), medical and surgical tests and treatments and medications diagnostic tests of any nature, and surgical procedures of any nature.

4. Nutrition and Hydration. If any attending physician shall state in writing that I am, to a reasonable degree of medical certainty, in a terminal condition or a permanently unconscious state, and that the provision (or continued provision) of nutrition and hydration will not, to a reasonable degree of medical certainty, prolong my life in accordance with my wishes, provide comfort to me, or minimize my pain or discomfort, then I authorize and direct that the provision of further nutrition or hydration may cease.

I AGREE TO ABOVE NUTRITION/HYDRATION PROVISION:

_____

*YOUR NAME

5.   Medication and Treatments to Alleviate Pain and Suffering.

a. Even if procedures and treatments are to be withheld or withdrawn, I wish that all palliative treatment and measures for my comfort, and to alleviate my pain, be continued.

b. Such efforts to relieve pain may be continued even if such measures may: shorten my life, lead to permanent addiction, have potentially dangerous ancillary consequences, render me unconscious, or lead to permanent physical damage.

6. Wishes Concerning Living Arrangements.

a. **Comment:** *Elaborate and provide detail, discuss hospice care arrangements.*

b. It is my wish that I live in my home rather than a institution, hospital, nursing home, or other facility, if such an arrangement would not jeopardize the chance of a meaningful recovery, impose undue burden on my family, or prevent my obtaining maximum pain relief for any illness from which I suffer.

c. Although I have some preference to reside in my home with care, if no family member is living with me, and only hired help can be obtained, I request that my Agent, in my Agent's discretion, weigh the benefits of such an environment to that of a better health care facility, if available. By way of example and not limitation, the services and socialization of a health care facility should be considered.

7. Transfer or Removal to Another Health Care Facility.

a. In the event that any health care facility in which I am located is unwilling or unable to carry out my Wishes, I authorize my being moved to another health care facility, even one located in a different state (and to facilitate such a removal I expressly authorize that the laws of such other state may be designated to govern this document). I direct that my health care providers cooperate with, and assist in, promptly transferring me to another health care facility if necessary for my care or to carry out my Wishes.

b. I further direct my medical care provider to transfer a copy of all of my medical records with me in such instance. This authorization to release medical records, to any health care facility to which I am transferred, is expressly intended to constitute a full authorization and release under HIPAA of any such information, including but not limited to private health information. I specifically indemnify and hold harmless any medical care facility releasing me and my records for such purpose.

8. Careful Consideration Has Been Made of Decisions in This Document.

a. These decisions and requests are made after careful consideration and reflection.

b. These decisions are made to avoid the indignity, pain and difficulties, both for myself and my family, of prolonged, hopeless deterioration and dependence where I am in a condition described above.

9. Religious Convictions: General Statement.

a. **Option 1:** *No Religious Restrictions Should Apply.* I do not wish to condition the effectiveness of this directive upon its conforming to any *RELIGION or other religious doctrines or beliefs to which I may be believed to subscribe.

b. **Option 2:** *Religious Principles Shall Apply to the Interpretation of This Living Will.* I wish to condition the effectiveness of this directive upon its conforming to *RELIGION doctrines and beliefs to which I subscribe. In order to effectuate my Wishes, if any question arises as to the requirements of my religious beliefs, I direct that the guidance of a religious advisor selected in accordance with my statement of religious beliefs made in this paragraph be sought.

10. Organ Donation. *Comment:* *If you have a chronic or other Illness you may wish to provide for a specific donation of organs or tissues to permit research to combat that health problem. The following is an illustrative clause that can be modified for your health issues.* Because I have lived for many decades with Multiple Sclerosis I expressly include this provision directing the donation of brain or central nervous system ("CNS") tissue samples for MS research efforts, but for no other purpose. I expressly note and acknowledge that my core religious preferences may mandate against organ donations, nevertheless, I expressly wish to provide for these tissue donations in spite of any such strictures.

11. Funeral and Related Arrangements.

a. ***Comment***: *Select, modify, or provide guidance as to funeral and other last arrangements. Consider the provisions as possible suggestions.*

b. *Religious Principles Shall Apply to Funeral and Other Arrangements.* Notwithstanding any statements above concerning inapplicability of religious doctrines, I specifically request that:

(1) My funeral service and arrangements and burial be in accordance with *RELIGION religious customs.

(2) A burial plot and marker may be purchased in accordance with my wishes, and to make such other arrangements as are appropriate, if I have not already done so myself.

(3) Cremation, and internment of my remains, including the purchase of a place of internment.

12. No Time Limit; Duration. I have considered the possibility of limiting the effectiveness of this instrument to a fixed period of time from the date hereof and have decided that it shall remain in full force and effect for as long as I may live. This Living Will may be so relied upon by any person or institution unless such person or institution has actually received a written notice of revocation or change.

13. Morally Binding. These directions are the exercise of my right to refuse treatment. Therefore, I expect my family, physicians, and all those concerned with my care to regard themselves as legally (whether of not required by the law at the time of the execution, or the place of implementation, of this Living Will) and morally bound to act in accordance with these directions. In doing so they will be free from any liability and responsibility for having followed my Wishes.

14. Revocation of Prior Grants. This document revokes any prior living will, executed by me.

15. Copies of Document. A copy, facsimile, PDF, or other electronic transmission or copy of an executed version of this document shall be as valid as the original. I ask that a copy of this document be made part of my permanent medical record.

16. Competency to Execute Documents. I understand the full import of this document and I am emotionally and mentally competent to execute it.

17. Construction and Interpretation of This Document.

a. The provisions of this entire document are separable so that the invalidity of one or more provisions shall not affect any others.

b. Should legislation or regulations be enacted after the execution of this Living Will, then this Living Will shall, to the extent necessary to make it valid and enforceable, be interpreted so as to comply with such future legislation or regulations in the manner which most closely approximates my Wishes.

c. Any titles and captions contained in this article are for convenience only and should not be read to affect the meaning of any provision.

IN WITNESS WHEREOF, I have executed this declaration *MONTH *DAY, *YEAR.

_____

*YOUR NAME

Witness: _____

State of *STATE-EXECUTION

County of *COUNTY NAME)

On this *MONTH *DAY, *YEAR, before me, the subscriber, a notary of the State of *STATE-EXECUTION, personally appeared *YOUR NAME who, I am satisfied after inspection of *STATENAME driver's license, is the principal mentioned in, and who signed the Living Will and acknowledged that he or she signed, sealed and delivered the same as his or her act and deed, that he or she appeared to be of sound mind and not under any duress, fraud or undue influence, and for the uses and purposes therein expressed.

_____

Notary Signature

DECLARATION OF WITNESSES TO LIVING WILL FOR MEDICAL DECISIONS

The undersigned each hereby declare and attest that: (1) the Living Will was personally signed, sealed, and delivered by *YOURNAME, in my presence, and I, at *YOUR NAME's request and in *YOUR NAME's presence and in the presence of the other witnesses, I subscribed my name as a witness; (2) I did not sign the signature of *YOUR NAME; (3) I am acquainted with *YOUR NAME and believe *YOUR NAME to be of sound mind and under no constraint, duress or undue influence; (4) I am not related to *YOUR NAME by blood or marriage; (5) I am not, to the best of my knowledge, entitled to any portion of the estate of *YOUR NAME under any Will of *YOUR NAME or Codicil now existing, nor am I so entitled by operation of law; (6) I do not have any present or inchoate claim against any portion of *YOUR NAME's estate or for *YOUR NAME's medical care; (7) I am not a physician attending to *YOUR NAME as a patient; and (8) I am over eighteen (18) years of age.

Printed Name of Witness	Address (City and State) of Witness	Signature of Witness

CHAPTER 8

EMERGENCY CHILD MEDICAL FORM

WHAT IS AN EMERGENCY CHILD MEDICAL FORM?

THERE IS A GAP IN MOST ESTATE PLANS concerning minor children. Guardian appointments under a will take effect only after the death of the parents. So if your child is in the hands of a caregiver, and you're mountain climbing or on safari and cannot be reached, important personal or medical information about the child may not be known in case of an emergency. This applies to all parents, but it may apply even more to those who are living with a chronic illness.

Your living will addresses your health care matters. But if you are unable to make medical decisions for your child because of the impact of your chronic illness or if you are hospitalized, who will make decisions concerning your child's medical treatment? Hopefully, a relative or trusted family friend will step in and take the child to a doctor or emergency room. But this person may know nothing at all about the child's medical history or other important facts. It is for this reason that creating and signing an emergency child medical form is so critical. It is an instrument that can protect your child in many ways. By filling out this form, you can make provisions to ensure that your child will be cared for correctly and appropriately. The form in the appendix following this chapter does not have any guaranteed legal validity, but it can prove quite helpful in an emergency (and it sure beats the handwritten note many people write before leaving to catch an airplane).

However, the form's usefulness will depend on the thoroughness with which you fill it out, your communication with your child's (or other minor ward's) pediatrician, your instructions to the caregiver, and so on.

WHO SHOULD HAVE ONE?

Any parent with minor children should fill out an emergency child medical form. You may also want to fill it out if you are the primary caregiver for stepchildren, or even foster children, or if you are guardian of a niece or nephew. In fact, any child whom you take care of should be protected. The emergency child medical form is a very good way to address this issue, especially if no one else is familiar with a child's medical information. It is not alright to assume that your spouse or sibling or someone else in the family will know what to do or be around to do it. While this is not intended to frighten readers, accidents do happen and if the person you thought would take care of things suddenly dies or is incapacitated, the child may have no one left who can attend to this. Consider the form as an indispensable, worst-case scenario backup plan. There is a very good likelihood that the worst-case scenario will never occur, but you've lost nothing by taking precautions.

WHAT INFORMATION SHOULD BE INCLUDED?

The more information you include on this form, the easier you will make it for your children to be protected and for their caregivers to act. You must include the name of the agent you have chosen to take care of your child (or children) in your place, with all contact information available. You should also list several successor agents, along with their contact information. Supply all appropriate medical insurance information for your children, and note each child's blood type, allergies, existing medical conditions, and any current medications. The form should also include a detailed medical history, any possible religious restrictions, and any additional information you feel your child's caregiver should have. If your child has a unique medical situation, it is crucial that this be noted so that medical care can be addressed appropriately.

WHAT HAPPENS AFTER YOU SIGN THE FORM?

Once you sign this form, one original should be given to the primary caregiver for your child if you are absent. Another original should be given to your children's pediatrician. One original remains in your home.

CHAPTER SUMMARY

If you are living with a chronic illness and have a minor child, you need to take extra precautions to protect your child if an emergency arises. You may have to make certain that your caregivers, family members, or friends are informed of key information that can be useful if the child becomes sick or is injured at a time when you are incapable of dealing with the crisis. Prepare and sign an emergency child medical form and give copies to the child's pediatrician and to other people who might be involved in caring for the child if you cannot. This should be done well in advance of any emergency arising. The appendix that accompanies this chapter provides you with a sample form to use. If your situation deteriorates to the point where you cannot care for your child, a guardian may have to be appointed.

AUTHORIZATION FOR
EMERGENCY CARE OF MINOR CHILD
INSTRUCTIONS

Medical Authorization Form Instructions: There is a gap in most estate plans concerning minor children. Guardian appointments under a will only take effect on the death of the parents. The parents' living wills only address the parents' health care matters. If the parents are on vacation, not reachable or disabled, who can make a decision concerning a child's medical and related treatment? Also, when the child is in the hands of a caregiver and the parents cannot be reached, important personal or medical information may not be known. This form attempts to address this gap.

Parents and others responsible for minors should be aware that this "form" does not have any guaranteed legal validity; it is not sanctioned by any statute or other legal authority. It may prove helpful. However, its usefulness will depend on the thoroughness with which you fill it out, your communication with your child's (or other minor ward's) pediatrician, your instructions to the caregiver, and so on. The form is a start, but just that.

If the parent has a chronic illness or health issue that may affect his or her ability to render care to a minor child, this form could be of great importance. In such situations, note this fact in the document. Perhaps you may be reached by phone but cannot accompany the child to an emergency room or other medical appointment because of incapacity.

If the child has a known health issue, it should be addressed in the document.

✵ ✵ ✵ ✵ ✵

A. Authorization by Parent(s) to Care For Children. I *CLIENT NAME and *SPOUSENAME (collectively and individually "Parent"), residing at *CLIENT ADDRESS, make, and declare this my medical authorization, directive and instruction (my "Authorization") concerning the care of *CHILDREN'S NAMES (individually and collectively "Child").

B. Agent Shall be Deemed In Loco Parentis to Child. It is my express intent, and I hereby authorize, the Agent named herein, to act as, and be treated by all medical providers as acting, in loco parentis for my Child.

C. Agent to Authorize Medical Care for Child. In the event that I am not Available in the event of a medical need, I authorize and direct that any doctor, hospital, emergency room facility, ambulance, or other medical care provider ("Medical Care Provider"), rely on the instructions of the first person in the following list who is able and willing and Available to act ("Agent"), in caring for any of the Child in a medical emergency, or until I can reasonably be contacted. *EXPLAIN PARENT HEALTH CONDITION THAT MAY MAKE PARENT'S PRESENCE UNLIKELY IN MANY EVENTS* If any person on the list below is not Available, the medical care provider should contact the next person. The term "Available" shall be determined in the reasonable discretion of the Medical Care Provider.

Name	Relationship	Home Address	Telephone Numbers
			Work: Home: Vacation: Cell:
			Work: Home: Vacation: Cell:
			Work: Home: Vacation: Cell:

D. Insurance Coverage.

Insurance Carrier Name	
Name of Insured	
Policy Number	

E. Guardian and Conservator. To the extent that I am permitted by law to do so, and subject to the terms of my will, I hereby nominate *TEMPORARY GUARDIAN NAME* to serve as my child's temporary guardian, temporary medical guardian, conservator, or in any similar representative capacity. Such request governs guardianship over the person(s) not property. If I am not permitted by law to so nominate, then I request that any court that may be involved in the appointment of a guardian, special medical guardian, conservator, or similar representative for me, give the greatest weight to this request. In the event of my demise, the terms of my will shall govern.

F. Agents Authorized to Access Confidential Medical Information.

1. I expressly authorize the release of any medical information concerning my Child to my Agent, or any recipient designated by my Agent, including but not limited to private health information ("PHI").

2. I authorize my Agent to request, obtain, receive, and inspect any and all information bearing upon my Child's health and relevant to any determinations to be made respecting any health care decision (including, but not limited to, all medical treatments and procedures), to sign whatever authorizations for release of information which may be required by providers or others, and to waive any rights I may have for breach of confidentiality for the release of such information to my Agent. I intend for my Agent to be treated as I would with regard to the use and dissemination of my Child's individually identifiable health information and medical records. This authority applies to any information governed by the Health Insurance Portability and Accountability Act of 1996 ("HIPAA"), 42 USC 132d and 45 CFR 160-164. I specifically authorize, on behalf of my Child, any physician, dentist, health care professional, medical provider, health plan, hospital, clinic, laboratory, pharmacy, or other covered health care provider, any insurance company and the Medical Information Bureau Inc., or any other health care organization that has provided treatment or services to me or that has paid for or is seeking payment from me for such services to give, disclose, and release to my Agent all of my individually identifiable health information and medical records regarding any past, present, or future medical or mental health condition.

G. Powers and Rights of Agents.

1. To make all necessary arrangements for my Child at any hospital, emergency room, or other health care facility, or similar establishment, including the transfer and removal of my Child from one such facility to another, and any decision reasonably necessary to assure that all my Child's essential needs are provided for at such a facility.

2. To give or withhold consent or informed consent to any medical procedures, test, or treatment, including surgery, hospitalization, convalescent care, home care, or other treatment which I, my Child, or another person may have arranged for my Child. To summon paramedics or other emergency medical personnel and seek emergency treatment for my Child. Such may include by way of example and not limitation routine health care, administration of prescribed medication, ordering of routine tests (including but not limited to x-rays), arranging transportation to and from such medical care providers, and matters incident and related thereto.

3. The Agent shall be entitled to sign, execute, deliver, and acknowledge any contract or other document that may be necessary, desirable, convenient or proper in order to exercise any of the powers described in this Authorization and to incur reasonable costs in the carrying out of this Authorization.

4. The Agent, however, shall not be permitted to take the following actions or make the following decisions ("Exclusions") [If none listed no exclusions shall apply]:

<table>
<tr><td></td></tr>
<tr><td></td></tr>
<tr><td></td></tr>
</table>

H. No Time Limit. I have considered the possibility of limiting the effectiveness of this instrument to a fixed period of time from the date hereof and have decided that it shall remain in full force and effect until revoked.

I. Authorization and Direction Binding. I expect my family, physicians, and all those concerned with the care of my Child to regard themselves as legally (whether or not required by the law at the time of the execution, or the place of implementation, of this Authorization) and morally bound to act in accordance with these directions, and in so doing to be free from any liability and responsibility for having followed my wishes stated herein.

J. Third Parties. Third parties, including but not limited to medical professionals, insurance companies, hospitals, convalescent facilities, or the like, may rely upon the representations of an Agent as to all matters relating to any power granted to an Agent acting in the capacity as the Agent for my Child.

K. Construction. This Agreement shall be governed under the laws of the State of *STATE NAME. This Agreement may be executed in one or more counterparts. Should any provision contained in this Authorization be unenforceable, such unenforceability shall not affect the enforceability of the remainder of this Authorization. The use of male, female, singular, or plural, shall be interpreted as the usage requires.

Acknowledgement of Parent(*s) and Affidavits of Witnesses:

I, *CLIENT NAME and *SPOUSE NAME, being first duly sworn, do hereby declare that, I am the parent and legal guardian of the Child named in this Authorization, that I have executed this Authorization instrument willingly, as my free and voluntary act for the purposes herein expressed, that at the time of said execution I am Eighteen (18) years of age or older, of sound mind and under no constraint or undue influence.

_____   _____
*CLIENT NAME   *SPOUSE NAME

State of *STATE - EXECUTION

County of *COUNTY NAME

On this *MONTH *DAY *YEAR before me personally came, *CLIENT NAME and *SPOUSE NAME, the Parent, known to me to be the individual described in and who executed the foregoing Authorization in my presence. The Parent duly acknowledged, subscribed and swore before me that he or she understood the meaning of the Authorization and executed the same before me.

_____
Notary Public

MEDICAL HISTORY AND RELATED INFORMATION

	Child 1 Name	Child 2 Name	Child 3 Name	Child 4 Name	Child 5 Name
Blood Type					
Allergies					
Existing Medical Conditions					
Medications Taken					
Child's Past Medical History					
Smoke / Drink / Drug Use					
Family Medical History					
Religious Restrictions on Care					
Child's Social History					
Other Comments					
Tips on How to Comfort Child (favorite toys, etc.)					

CHAPTER 9

YOUR WILL
DISTRIBUTING ASSETS AND CARING FOR YOUR LOVED ONES

WHY YOUR WILL IS NOT THE FOCUS OF THIS BOOK

ASK ALMOST ANYONE ABOUT ESTATE PLANNING and the first, and often only, step mentioned is preparing a will. So why is your will, if it is so important, not the focus of this book? The answer is simple. The focus of this book is on planning for those with chronic illness and is focused on providing guidance for those living with chronic illness and their loved ones to address and custom tailor estate planning in a sensitive and rational manner. While your will is an essential part of your estate plan, and possibly the key document governing the distribution of your assets on death and the appointment of a guardian if you have minor children, it is not much different from wills executed by people who do not have to contend with a chronic illness. Because the format (and use) of wills is generally the same for you as it is for other people, this chapter will be shorter and simpler than others in this book. You can generally rely on other general publications that deal with the issue of wills in greater detail.

A few points should be considered as to the differences you, as result of your chronic illness, may face with respect to your will:

❖   Planning to manage your assets for the duration of your life, especially if you are likely to experience cognitive impairment, will likely diminish the importance of your will. This is because the manner in which you own (title) assets may be modified to facilitate management of your affairs. A funded revocable living trust will make your will less important to the disposition of your assets upon your death. (See Chapters 10.)

❖　　You should consider making a bequest to charitable organizations dedicated to serving those living with the chronic illness you have and to providing research for a cure of that illness. It should be noted that many people who suffer from a chronic disease develop an unwavering drive to cure the disease. It is for this reason that, if you have the financial wherewithal to provide charitable support to a charity or foundation that has helped you, you are encouraged to help others.

❖　　Although your will may not have any unusual provisions, if your family or loved ones draft wills, their wills may need to be modified to include a special needs trust for you, as warranted.

What Is a Will?

A will, or Last Will and Testament, is a document in which you (the testator) state how your money and assets are to be distributed upon your death. Your will can also appoint an executor, who is a person that is responsible for managing your estate. Through your will, you appoint guardians to care for any minor children you may have. You can also name trustees to handle any trusts you may have set up in your will (a testamentary trust).

Everyone needs a will, and you are no exception. Even if you own assets jointly or fund a living trust, there is no assurance that some assets will not be governed by those arrangements. Your will may determine how your money is distributed on your death, but it can also accomplish much more. A properly prepared and executed will can protect your loved ones and ensure that your wishes are carried out.

Assets Not Affected by Your Wills

Many assets you own will not be distributed under your will. These may include:

❖　　IRA and other retirement plans, which have beneficiary designation forms that govern the passing of those assets to the people you name.

❖　　Life insurance policies, which are typically paid to the persons you name in the policy application (or a beneficiary change form you sign later), not by your will.

❖　　Jointly owned assets, such as a bank account that reads "John Smith and Jane Doe, as joint tenants with rights of survivorship," which pass to Jane on John's death without regard to a will.

❖　　Some bank and other accounts can be owned in a manner that transfers ownership on death outside of your will, such as a "pay on death" or "in trust for" account. For example, "John Smith, in trust for Jane Doe" or "John Smith, pay on death to, Jane Doe" will pass to Jane automatically on John's death.

❖　　If you use a revocable living trust to provide for your care, assets held by that trust will not pass under your will, but rather as directed by the trust document.

The fact that many, most, or even all of your assets pass outside of your will reflects the danger you face if you buy a cheap will from a web site. Such sites will not address the overall planning and relevance of your will in the context of your assets, goals, etc. What you really need is an estate planning specialist who is experienced in dealing with such matters. A professionally prepared will probably cost more than an online will, but the "great deal" is likely to create significant problems if title to your assets, beneficiary designations, and your will are not coordinated.

WHAT TO INCLUDE IN YOUR WILL

Your will should include the standard basic information most wills include: who your assets will be distributed to (spouse, partner, children, or friends) and the manner you want them distributed (outright transfer, trusts, at specific ages, etc.). You can also use your will to appoint a guardian for your minor children. You will name the executor of your will, who will manage the winding up of your personal financial matters, collect your assets, pay final bills and taxes, and distribute the remaining assets to your heirs. You can also name the trustees who will be handling the financial aspects of any trusts set up to manage assets for your hairs.

CHAPTER SUMMARY

This chapter has provided a brief overview of what your will is, some of the items to include in your will, and the few ways your will be might differ from those who are not living with a chronic illness. You should take advantage of the many available books and resources that focus on wills to learn more; generally, will planning applicable to the public at large also applies to you.

CHAPTER 10

REVOCABLE LIVING TRUST
MAINTAINING CONTROL AND PROTECTING YOU THROUGH DISABILITY

A REVOCABLE LIVING TRUST: THE MOST IMPORTANT DOCUMENT YOU MAY EVER SIGN

A REVOCABLE LIVING TRUST (sometimes called a "living trust," "loving trust," or "revocable inter vivos trust") might be the most powerful and beneficial tool to assist you in managing assets and other matters throughout the often unpredictable course of your disease. If you have the resources to afford a revocable living trust, it may end up being the most important document you ever sign. Careful attention, however, has to be given to this type of planning, and especially in your use of other materials made available to the public on living trusts. The reason for this is that almost all materials on living trusts focus on avoiding probate (the process of administering your will and assets following death).

As explained in Chapter 9, the manner in which you dispose of assets on death is really not different from the manner anyone else would use. Avoiding probate is rarely the big deal most books and "authorities" make it sound to be, but regardless, it is not an issue unique to you. Your living trust, on the other hand, should be a document planned and tailored to provide careful management of your assets during your life. This is especially important if your chronic illness progresses in a manner that diminishes and perhaps eliminates your ability to manage your own affairs. The type of living trust you need has a very different focus from the ones typically used and sold to the general public. This chapter will explain the technique and document, but will limit its focus to the matters most important to you. Therefore, you will need to supplement the information provided here with materials of a more general nature.

SOME REVOCABLE LIVING TRUST JARGON

A basic review of some of the legal jargon used in connection with a revocable living trust will make it easier for you to understand the discussions that follow:

❖   A living trust is a trust that you set up during your lifetime. In legal jargon, a "living" trust is often referred to as an "inter vivos" trust.

❖   In legal jargon, you are called the "trustor," "grantor," or "settler."

❖   A "trust" is a legal contract, made between you and the trustees, to accomplish the purposes stated in the document (called the "trust" or the "trust indenture").

❖   The "trustees" are the persons charged with managing the trust assets (called "corpus") for the purposes stated in the trust document. The trustees are "fiduciaries," people occupying a position of trust and held to a high standard of care and responsibility under the law.

❖   The trustees manage the trust assets for the people the trust document lists as benefiting from the trust. These people are referred to as "beneficiaries."

❖   Living trusts are almost always structured to be "revocable." This means that you can change your living trust at any time. This standard definition, however, leaves out a vital concept for you in light of your chronic illness. If your competency wanes to a point where you no longer have "contractual capacity" (a higher standard than mere testamentary capacity to sign a will), you will no longer be able to change your trust document. It will then become irrevocable. So, while your living trust may be revocable for a time, it may become irrevocable well before most living trusts. Depending on the course of your illness, your living trust may well be irrevocable throughout most of its use.

WHAT IS A REVOCABLE LIVING TRUST?

As noted above, a living trust is a trust that you set up during your lifetime.

You retain complete control over the assets in the trust while you are alive and competent. If you become unable to manage the trust, because of disability, hospitalization, or other issues, an alternate or "successor" trustee takes over managing your trust assets. This is an important point that warrants emphasis. The trustee of your living trust has no control over any assets not specifically included in your trust. So if you will be relying on your trust for protection, you need to transfer the assets that will afford this protection to your trust (called "funding").

The trustees of your trust are permitted to act only for the benefit of the beneficiaries of the trust, in accordance with the terms of the trust agreement. Although you may be the primary beneficiary, you don't have to be the only beneficiary. You can name other loved ones as beneficiaries too. Even if funds in the trust can only be used for your care during your lifetime, they will be distributed to your named heirs following your death. Most revocable trusts are drafted with the grantor of the trust (you) as the sole trustee. Because of your chronic illness, however, it might be better for you to name a cotrustee at the inception (creation) of the trust. If and when you are no longer capable of handling your own affairs, your cotrustee will be able to act on your behalf with a wide range of powers, solely with the purpose of benefiting you. Naming a cotrustee prevents time-consuming and convoluted impediments to carrying out your wishes and ensures that someone has the legal right to access and manage your assets to best provide for you.

For tax purposes, the trust is generally ignored and all income and deductions are reported on your own tax return. Because there is no current tax benefit of setting up a living trust, the format used can be quite flexible so it is adaptable to meet a broad range of your personal objectives.

On your death, provisions that serve the same purpose as a will apply to govern the disposition of your assets.

WHY YOU SHOULD HAVE A REVOCABLE LIVING TRUST

A revocable living trust may be the ideal vehicle for someone suffering from a chronic disease. It allows for the most comprehensive, detailed planning for any disability. In the appropriate circumstances, living trusts can be an ideal vehicle to serve your needs throughout the course of your chronic disease. Because of your chronic disease, it is possible that you may often require assistance and support with your financial affairs. If you have a disease course punctuated by frequent exacerbations, you may need someone to step in and assist you on a sporadic basis. In this event, having a revocable living trust and a successor or cotrustee can be ideal. This arrangement enables your cotrustee to act immediately, and to use your funds for your benefit. While your agent under your power of attorney can also do this, having a cotrustee of a revocable living trust allows all necessary actions to occur more quickly, easily, and effectively. A bank and other institutions will more readily accept the signature of a cotrustee than that of an agent acting in your name. This can facilitate carrying out your important personal objectives and offers you the best protection.

A living trust may also be a good idea for someone who does not have an adequate safety net of relatives or close friends to rely upon. With a living trust, you can name a bank or trust company as sole or cotrustee. The benefit to this is that a bank or trust company brings integrity, independence, and professionalism to the management of your trust and affairs. An institution won't serve as agent under your power of attorney.

WHO SHOULD NOT HAVE A REVOCABLE LIVING

A revocable living trust is not for everyone. If you cannot afford the cost of an attorney who specializes in estate planning to draft the trust, it may not be worthwhile to pursue this option. If you do not have significant assets to transfer to your revocable living trust, there is probably no need to create a trust of this kind. You might be quite wealthy, but if your assets are primarily in retirement accounts and life insurance policies, there may be little if any assets you can transfer to a trust.

HOW YOUR CHRONIC DISEASE AFFECTS YOUR REVOCABLE LIVING TRUST

As was explained in Chapter 4 of this book, the level of competency required to sign a trust contract is much higher than the level of capacity required to sign a will. Because of this high level of competency requirement, it is advisable to establish your trust early on, so that any possible cognitive symptoms of your chronic disease cannot be used to challenge the trust. The trust can be challenged on the basis of undue influence, mental incompetence, or lack of advice from independent counsel. Mental incompetence can be established from the testimony of physicians and others who provide treatment. Creating and signing the trust too late may make its validity questionable.

Revocable trusts are an ideal technique to assist many people living with a chronic illness to manage assets. However, as with the durable power of attorney discussed in Chapter 5, there are special nuances for you to consider. The typical revocable trust is drafted with the grantor as sole trustee. But if you have advanced Parkinson's or Alzheimer's, it may be best if you are not named a trustee at all. If, on the other hand, your disease is in the early stage or there is no significant cognitive impact, you may be best served by a hybrid approach. Instead of serving as a sole initial trustee to be replaced in the event of disability, or not serving at all, consider serving as an initial cotrustee. If you are the sole trustee and experience an exacerbation (something that typically occurs with MS), it might prove problematic. Not naming yourself as trustee at all, however, cedes control from you even though you will generally have the capacity to make decisions. Relying on a transition to a successor trustee not only creates the expected issues with triggering the transition (as with a springing power of attorney), but also results in your complete removal as trustee, which may be unwarranted.

Most people with a chronic illness want to resume their involvement as trustee when an exacerbation subsides. Thus, having another person serve along with you as cotrustees from inception is probably a wise choice. In addition, the trust document could state that either trustee alone should have the authority to act independently to take the actions that might be required during periods of an exacerbation or similar flare-up. This might include signature authority over banking matters, but might expressly exclude the right to sign an income tax return (but permit filing an extension or paying tax) or to sell an asset over some specified value. Significant decisions can be deferred until the exacerbation ends or expressly reserved to your discretion unless there is a permanent disability. The use of a cotrustee and this modification to typical trust language can provide an ideal solution for you and can give you maximum control while simultaneously creating a mechanism that ensures continuity during an unexpected attack.

Sample Provision

"Any trustee, acting alone and without any requirement for joint action, is authorized and permitted to make ministerial and administrative decisions, including, but not limited to, routine banking, investment, and brokerage transactions."

REVOCABLE LIVING TRUST HYPE AND FACT

A revocable trust is one of the most talked about estate planning techniques, but much of the talk is hype. Living trusts in the appropriate circumstances can be an ideal tool to accomplish many essential planning goals. In inappropriate circumstances, they can be an unnecessary waste of time and money, and create some unnecessary hassles and complications in managing your affairs. In a worse-case scenario you may use (or be sold) a revocable living trust when another technique would have been more appropriate. The results could be disastrous, especially if the planning ignores protecting you throughout the course of your chronic illness. Understanding how to look through the puffery will help you make better decisions:

❖ **Hype:** A living trust will solve all your problems.

❖ **Fact:** Slick sales pitches and canned documents will not address your specific needs. You need a document tailored to your personal situation, prepared by an attorney that specializes in estate planning.

EXAMPLE

Living trusts are often promoted at slick sales seminars, in some cases, not even presented by attorneys specializing in estate planning. After the scare tactics and donuts, you'll often be pressured to sign up for a "free" consultation. If you sign up for the living trust after the consultation, too often you'll wind up with prepackaged documents. Many of these marketing programs are often tied to larger companies that produce canned documents based on a generic questionnaire. The key problem for you with this approach is that the living trust documents you get will be very generic. More than likely they will be prepared by an attorney who is not an estate planning specialist and will focus more on avoiding probate than managing your life as your illness progresses. These companies may refuse (or lack the capability) to tailor the trust documents to the unique issues of your illness.

❖ **Hype:** A living trust avoids probate, the key problem.

❖ **Fact:** Living trusts, even when completed effectively with full consideration to your health concerns, will not solve all of your planning problems.

EXAMPLE

Assume you live in Vermont and have a rental vacation property in Pennsylvania. A living trust will avoid probate for the Pennsylvania property. (Avoiding probate is one of the purported great benefits of a living trust.) A living trust, however, will not facilitate making gifts of interests in that property to reduce your estate tax cost. A limited liability company (LLC) can achieve these two goals. Using a living trust instead of an LLC would be less than ideal. But it gets worse. If you use a living trust to avoid ancillary probate and are sued for more than your insurance coverage by an injured tenant (or your policy has an exception for the incident involved), your entire estate could be jeopardized. If instead you transferred the property to an LLC, you would limit your liability only to the property in question. Your home and other assets would be safe. Assuming the a living trust covers all contingencies can be disastrous.

❖ **Hype:** A living trust is necessary to avoid probate.

❖ **Fact:** Many people have the majority or even all of their assets pass outside of the probate process without a trust. Also, in most situations probate is really not that big a deal.

A living trust is primarily touted for its use as a method of avoiding probate. Probate, although it can be expensive in certain cases, is not necessarily the evil and excessively expensive process many people fear. Moreover, there are simple and no-cost ways to avoid probate when avoiding probate is appropriate. For example, naming your intended heirs as beneficiaries and not your estate avoids probate for insurance and retirement plans, and other assets. The appropriate ownership (title) of assets, as explained above, can also make probate unnecessary.

❖ **Hype:** Living trusts are simple, inexpensive, and easy.

❖ **Fact:** A living trust, especially when tailored to address the circumstances of your chronic illness, your needs, your objectives, etc., may not be simple or inexpensive (at least not if you want it to work).

A living trust is not necessarily the simple and inexpensive document many people expect (unless you use a cookie-cutter version like the one described earlier in this chapter). To properly set up a living trust, you must retain a lawyer to properly prepare a comprehensive plan and, based on that plan, a trust document. The trust document, if properly prepared, is not as simple as most sales pitches would have you believe. It is tailored to address your personal goals and objectives, estate tax (if any), and other needs. Be certain that the attorney you retain coordinates the tax allocation clause in your will with the tax clause in the trust. The trust document, however, is only step one. You should generally arrange to transfer many of your assets to the trust. For real estate, you will need to execute a deed and, depending on where you live, complete various tax and other forms. If the property has a mortgage, you will have to review the mortgage for a due-on-sale clause and most likely notify your bank. Insurance policies on real estate and art will have to be changed to the name of the trust to be effective. The title insurance company that insured any real estate you want to transfer to the living trust should be asked whether a new policy in the name of the trust is required. Personal property will require a bill of sale to effect transfer. Bank accounts should often be retitled into the name of your trust, and it might be advisable to obtain a separate tax identification number. Completing this process can be time consuming, can require the assistance of an attorney, and can create additional fees and charges, none of which would have to be incurred if you didn't set up the living trust. That doesn't mean avoid using a trust. Just do it right.

❖   **Hype:** A living trust is the only document you really need.

❖   **Fact:** A living trust will is never a substitute for a living will, health proxy, HIPAA release, or child medical emergency form discussed in prior chapters. If your planning (not just the trust document) is done well, a living trust can, to a large degree, substitute for a will and power of attorney. However, you still need these documents to ensure that no assets or rights are missed.

Using a living trust as a substitute for a will does not work for many reasons. For example, a will is often necessary to designate a guardian for minor children. You need a will because there is no assurance that every asset you currently own will be owned by your living trust at your death. This disparity could occur because of the improper or incomplete transfer of assets, acquisitions for which there was inadequate time to complete a transfer to your trust, assets which could not be assigned, and finally, assets that you may not be aware of existing (e.g., a lottery winning, won just before you check out!). If you have a living trust, however, your will might be reduced to a much shorter document called a "pour-over will." This type of will provides that all assets under the will are simply to be transferred to (or poured-over into) your living trust. Nevertheless, a fairly complete will is sometimes necessary to authorize your executor to take the actions that might be necessary if circumstances change, so it should include a full range of powers and other rights given to this executor.

Living wills and health care proxies are essential to address medical decisions if you are incapacitated. You need these documents whether or not you also have a living trust. The living trust used in conjunction with these documents can provide an even greater level of protection and perhaps minimize the likelihood of a guardianship proceeding. That could be especially important if your illness will likely result in a significant cognitive impairment.

A power of attorney also remains necessary. This designates someone to serve as your agent to handle legal, tax, and financial matters if you are disabled. You should have one even if you have a living trust to address assets and rights not transferred to the trust. It should be coordinated with the living trust to facilitate your agent transferring assets to the living trust if you are disabled.

❖   **Hype:** Living trusts are safer than wills.

❖   **Fact:** As explained earlier, especially in Chapter 4, living trusts are contracts and thus require a greater level of competency than that required to sign a will. Therefore, living trusts don't always prevent legal challenges, they may encourage them. If you are already suffering from cognitive impact because of your illness (e.g., mild dementia from Alzheimer's disease), the question as to the validity of a living trust must be evaluated by an attorney before you proceed to use this as a planning technique.

You can have the mental awareness (testamentary capacity) to sign a will but lack the required legal capacity to sign a living trust. A trust is a contract, so you must have the comprehension, understanding, and state of mind required to create one and have the assurance that it is (and will remain) legally binding. The standard that has been accepted by the law to sign a will has intentionally been made easier to enable people in extremis to sign wills. The standard to sign a will merely requires you to be aware of your descendants, the extent of your assets, and the fact that you are signing a document to bequeath those assets to the persons you name. If you are disabled or infirm, you may be legally incapable of signing a contract but still have sufficient capacity to sign a will. In such cases, a will might be the better, or even only, choice.

❖   **Hype:** Living trusts ensure confidentially; wills don't.

❖   **Fact:** If your estate is probated, there is no assurance of confidentiality, and a living trust does not preclude probate.

The claim that a living trust can enable you to minimize (not avoid) having your assets and wishes disclosed to the public is only a very small part of the story. Your will is a public document once probated. If your will contains a pour-over and is probated, the probate process may require that your living trust be recorded in the public record in a manner similar to recording your will. In addition, many states require the recording of a living trust in the same manner. If the living trust is challenged by a wanna-be beneficiary, the trust might easily wind up in court records, which are open to the public. Thus, in some cases, there may be little or no additional confidentiality offered by a living trust. That doesn't mean you shouldn't have one; it just means that you should be aware of its limitations and focus on its real, not hyped, benefits.

❖   **Hype:** Living trusts will dramatically save on legal fees by avoiding probate.

❖   **Fact:** Living trusts don't save on legal fees; proper planning does.

Remember that your focus should be on what your living trust will do to protect you throughout the course of your illness. Whether or not you save legal fees on probate is not the primary question. Nevertheless, since this is a purported benefit, it can be addressed. Legal fees will be incurred on death whether a will or living trust is used. When a person with a living trust dies, the assets in that trust must still be transferred to the designated beneficiaries. Additional trusts may have to be set up (e.g., the bypass trust for tax benefits, trusts for minor children, a dynasty trust, etc.). Thus, whether assets pass through probate or under a living trust, steps will still have to be taken to transfer those assets. If the property is real estate, stocks or other assets, the paperwork may not be that different. In many cases, it is actually possible to probate an estate for far lower legal costs than many popular books and articles in financial publications indicate. Numbers like 5 percent to 10 percent, or more, of total assets are often suggested as typical costs and fees for probating an estate. In many instances, this is a gross exaggeration. The size of the estate often has little to do with the amount of work involved in the probate process. The nature of the assets, the cooperation of family members, and the organization of necessary financial and personal records are important factors in determining the extent of the legal work involved. Moreover, the particular probate court that will handle the estate can have a significant effect on the overall cost of a probate. Many probate (surrogate) court officials are extremely efficient, helpful, and professional, and this can dramatically reduce the cost and time involved. If your estate is taxable, a federal estate tax return will have to be filed. Using a living trust does nothing to reduce the costs of this filing.

❖ **Hype:** Living trusts avoid taxes.

❖ **Fact:** Most of the claimed tax benefits are a sales pitch!

From an income tax perspective, living trusts are characterized as "grantor trusts." This means that the income and expenses of the trust appear on your personal tax return as if the trust did not exist. For the 2008 federal tax return, only estates in excess of $2 million were subject to estate tax. This figure increased to $3.5 million in 2009. Although the future of the estate tax is uncertain, one thing is clear. If you might even possibly be subject to a federal estate tax, you can well afford to get proper legal advice to plan for it. You shouldn't be relying on a book or any marketing pitch. The only estate tax benefit from a living trust is where other planning techniques, in particular gift powers and other trusts, are incorporated into a living trust. The living trust itself does not provide any tax benefit. These additional planning techniques are beyond the scope of this book and with perhaps one exception are identical to the planning techniques other taxpayers take. The key exception is that if your competency wanes as a result of your illness, you may not have the flexibility to revise your estate plan to address whatever form, if any, the estate tax will take in the future. You might in fact consider using a more sophisticated living trust document, one that gives considerably more flexibility to your trustees to modify tax aspects of your plan in the future if you are unable to do so.

EXAMPLE

Assume that your living trust provides that the first $2 million of your assets will be transferred to a bypass trust to benefit your surviving spouse (for the sake of clarity, let's assume this is a wife), which will then not be taxed in her estate. On your wife's death, her $1 million estate is protected by the exclusion of the $2 million transferred through the bypass trust (2008) and passes free of tax to your children. By protecting your exclusion, and by using your wife's exclusion, the estate tax is avoided through the provisions in your living trust. Your living trust, however, hasn't provided you any benefit that a will couldn't have provided.

FOUR STAGES IN THE LIFE OF YOUR LIVING TRUST: HOW A LIVING TRUST WORKS

The best way to understand how a living trust works is to review the four stages in the lifecycle of a typical revocable living trust.

PHASE 1: FORMATION

After a complete review of your tax, estate, financial, and personal goals and status, a comprehensive plan should be formulated. When a revocable living trust is an appropriate component of this plan, you should retain a lawyer to draft the trust. The trust should be signed, witnessed, and notarized. Copies of the trust should be given to your professional advisers and family. Assets should then be transferred to your trust.

PHASE 2: MANAGEMENT PRIOR TO YOUR BEING INCAPABLE OF ACTING AS TRUSTEE

Manage the assets in your trusts as if they were your own, with one twist—transactions affecting trust assets will be completed in the name of the trust. You will sign trust checks and buy stock in your trust's name. However, if your illness has progressed significantly before you establish your living trust, you might have to skip this step and go to Phase 3. As noted earlier, having a cotrustee at Phase 2 is a great way to provide protections for you, keep you in control of your finances as long as possible, and ease the transition to Phase 3 when it becomes necessary. Having a cotrustee and consolidating all appropriate assets into your living trust may so simplify your financial and legal matters that it will significantly prolong the time period during which you can retain control of your affairs.

PHASE 3: YOU BECOME INCAPABLE OF MANAGING YOUR AFFAIRS

When you become incapable of serving as a trustee of your trust, your successor trustees will take over the management of your trust assets.

Your agent, acting under your durable power of attorney, may transfer to your living trust any assets you own outside the trust. Your living trust should contain detailed provisions stating how and who should take over. The trust should make it clear how to determine that you are disabled so that your successor trustees can know when to take over. It should also indicate that if you recover, you can take back control of your financial management.

An important part of the disability provisions of your living trust is detailed instructions as to how you should be cared for in the event of disability. Many of the "form" trusts simply do not provide this type of personalized detail. Do you want to avoid being placed in a nursing home as long as possible? Do you have preferences for the type of health care facility in which you should be placed if it becomes absolutely necessary? If geographic preferences are important to you during your life, you should specify in your living trust that, in the event of your disability, you would wish to be placed in a facility located in a certain part of the country (perhaps near your family). If religious preferences are important, you may wish to specify that the health care facility be near a church, mosque, or synagogue so that you can attend services, or that the facility meets your religious dietary requirements. Do not assume that your trustees will know your preferences. Specifying such details may be critical, depending on who the trustees are. Details can also enable your trustees to respond to a challenge by your heirs as to the appropriateness of the decisions and expenditures they make.

PHASE 4: AFTER YOUR DEATH

On death, your trust becomes irrevocable and your successor trustees will carry out your wishes (e.g., funding a bypass trust). Any assets which were not already transferred to your trust (either by you when you formed the trust, at a later date by you, or by your agent under your durable power of attorney after your disability), can be transferred under what is known as a pour-over will. The key provision of this will provides that any assets that you may have owned at your death, which were not already in your trust, should be transferred (or poured over into) your living trust. Many different types of trusts can be incorporated into your living trust. Again, this type of planning is largely the same as for anyone and is not the focus of this book.

EXAMPLE • *Multiple Sclerosis*

Assume you have progressive-remitting multiple sclerosis (MS). There will be periods of time, perhaps most of the time, when you can manage your affairs. However, during an exacerbation, you'll likely need assistance. As time goes on and your disabilities worsen, it will likely be helpful to have a cotrustee who can handle some of the administrative matters that you cannot handle. A revocable trust might be the most appropriate tool to handle this contingency.

If you are married or have a partner, it might be assumed that your spouse or partner should be the obvious sole successor trustee, this is not always advisable. The burden of being a caregiver for you as your MS progresses can be substantial, and providing assistance for the caregiver with a cotrustee, perhaps an institutional trustee than can relieve the caregiver of investment, distribution, check writing, and other burdens, may be ideal. If the caregiver is a friend and not a spouse, the insulation from claims by using an institutional trustee, especially in light of the other burdens the friend/caregiver carries, could be invaluable. If a bank or trust company serves as cotrustee, their involvement will insulate your partner or friend who serves as cotrustee from a variety of potential lawsuits.

The revocable trust should provide for a clear mechanism to determine if or when you should cease serving as trustee. If you are serving as a cotrustee with an institution and have funded the trust with most of your assets, that day will be put off as long as feasible and may never arrive. The language often used to accomplish this in many trust documents might be inappropriate to you in light of your MS. Merely being "disabled" may not be a relevant criteria. You may be "disabled" from the date the trust is first signed, but still be quite capable of managing your financial and other affairs. Other disability triggers are inappropriate because even though you may be disabled during an exacerbation, following that exacerbation you may again be perfectly capable of managing your affairs. While some trusts use an on/off mechanism of providing that when the grantor/trustee recovers from a disability he or she will again resume being a trustee, this approach is also inadequate. The mechanisms may be too burdensome, the definitions may not address MS, and timing issues may create problems. The specific definitions under which a successor trustee can demonstrate your inability to serve as trustee should be tailored to reflect the nuances of your illness, any cognitive impairment, and so on.

You should be encouraged to address with some detail the care and living arrangements you desire to provide guidance to the successor trustees. This might include personal details as to where and how you would like to live, etc.

CHAPTER SUMMARY

This chapter has explored the revocable living trust, a document that can be the most important estate and financial planning tool to manage your affairs and ensure that you are protected throughout the course of your illness. However, as with all estate planning documents, you must carefully tailor this document to address your unique situation, and your chronic illness in particular.

SAMPLE REVOCABLE LIVING TRUST
PROVISIONS FOR THOSE WITH CHRONIC ILLNESS

[**CAUTION:** This is not a complete trust, just selected provisions.
See www.laweasy.com for a complete sample document.]

1. **Distributions [Selected provisions].**

    a. Distributions During Grantor's Lifetime - Grantor Not Disabled.

        i. During Grantor's lifetime when the Grantor is not disabled:

            1. The Trustee shall hold the Trust Estate, in trust, to pay or apply to or for the benefit of any one or more of the following persons: Grantor, Grantor's children (which shall include *CHILDREN NAMES, and any children born or legally adopted after the execution of this Trust Agreement, collectively "Children," individually "Child"), but not Grantor's grandchildren or later descendants (collectively these are referred to as "Recipients"). The net income of the Trust shall be applied in amounts, whether equal or unequal, as the Trustee (or the Independent Trustee where applicable), in the exercise of discretion, may consider desirable for the health, education, support, or maintenance, to maintain the Recipient's in accordance with the Standard for Payment defined below. The judgment of the Trustee, as to the propriety and amount of such payment, shall be conclusive.

            2. It is the express desire of the Grantor that the Trustee apply income liberally, and primarily for the care of Grantor and in a manner to maintain Grantor's historic lifestyle and activities to the extent feasible and practical in light of Grantor's current and future health status. These decisions shall be made without concern for the retention of any monies for future or remainder beneficiaries.

            3. The Trustee may accumulate any of the net income not paid or applied for the benefit of the Recipients, and add it to the principal of this Trust at least annually and thereafter to hold, administer, and dispose of it as a part of the Trust Estate.

        ii. Distributions During Grantor's Life - Grantor Disabled.

            1. During Grantor's disability, as defined below, the Trustee shall administer the Trust Estate for the care of Grantor, and shall expend any amounts of Trust income or principal as the Trustee, in the exercise of discretion, shall deem necessary or advisable in accordance with the following provisions.

            2. During any disability of the Grantor, the Grantor directs that the no restrictions shall apply as to distributions to or for the benefit of Grantor. Grantor directs that during Grantor's disability:

            a. Grantor directs that Grantor have the best medical and health care provided to Grantor and that the Trustee shall distribute Trust income and principal accordingly. The term "best" shall be defined, to the extent feasible and applicable based on the caliber of medical care that Grantor sought prior to being deemed disabled under the provisions of this Trust, adjusted to reflect the current status of Grantor's health. Notwithstanding the foregoing, the Trustee is directed to pay for and to the extent feasible actively seek out experimental and new medical therapies to help Grantor's condition, including but not limited to alternative treatments that have received positive reviews in medical literature.

            b. Grantor directs that every effort reasonable be made to enable Grantor to continue to reside in Grantor's personal residence for as long as practical, and that every reasonable effort be made to accommodate Grantor's health care needs in such home rather than relocating to a health care facility.

            c. In the event that Grantor must be relocated to any nursing or health care facility, Grantor directs that every effort possible be made that any such facility:

                i. Be operated under *RELIGIOUS PREFERENCE auspices.

                ii. Have *DESCRIBE food service facilities, and where possible have, or be within reachable distance to a *RELIGION house of worship.

            d. Notwithstanding anything in this Trust to the contrary, any restrictions on distributions provided in the provision below governing "Distributions To A Person Under A Disability," shall not apply to restrict any distributions to Grantor when Grantor is disabled, or following any period of Grantor's disability [Note: Many trust documents include additional restrictions on distributions to a beneficiary who is disabled. In this context, those would be generic provisions to apply in the event an heir who receives funds from the trust is disabled. Those provisions would not be tailored to address your situation, so they are made inapplicable to you].

3. Short Duration Disability from Which Recovery Is Anticipated.

a. Because Grantor is living with *CHRONIC ILLNESS, it is anticipated that periodically Grantor may suffer a short term attack or exacerbation. The Grantor directs that, barring an emergency situation which cannot await Grantor's recuperation or recovery from such attack or exacerbation, that the disability provisions in this Trust shall not be applied so long as the period for which it is anticipated that Grantor will not be able to reasonably participate in the management of this Trust shall be less than Thirty (30) days. This condition shall be referred to as an "Ignored Disability."

b. However, in the event that an institutional cotrustee is serving and such institutional trustee [Note: Modify if you are not using an institution, but consider if you wish to grant this authority to a non-institutional trustee] determines in its absolute discretion that Grantor must be replaced to address an important or emergency situation.

c. In the event of Grantor being subject to an Ignored Disability, a confirmation by any of Grantor's attending physicians in writing that Grantor is subject to an Ignored Disability as defined above shall suffice to confirm such status.

4. Determination of Grantor's Disability.

a. The Grantor shall be deemed to be disabled when Grantor is unable to manage Grantor's affairs and property effectively for reasons such as mental illness, mental deficiency, physical illness or disability, advanced age, chronic use of drugs, chronic intoxication, confinement, kidnapping, detention by a foreign power or disappearance, or for any other reason allowable by statute or law. Grantor expressly states that Grantor presently has *CHRONIC ILLNES and has the following conditions and symptoms *DESCRIBE SYMPTOMS. Further, Grantor anticipates that *FUTURE SYMPTOMS are likely to occur. So long as Grantor, with the assistance and guidance of the Institutional Cotrustee [Note: If you don't use an institutional Cotrustee, modify and rethink this] is able to reasonably participate in the management and decision making under this trust, regardless of *DESCRIBE ACCEPTABLE LIMITATIONS, shall remain a Cotrustee hereunder and shall not be deemed disabled. [Note: The objective is to tailor the definition of "disability" so that you are only replaced as a trustee when you really should be. Unless you address the nuances of your situation, that decision won't be made at the appropriate time].

b. In addition to any other method acceptable to any third party relying upon the effectiveness of the appointment of any Trustee or successor Trustee, or any method allowed by law, it shall be deemed conclusive proof that the appointment of such person is effective upon a written statement being executed by each of Grantor's neurologist [OTHER SPECIALIST] and primary care physician or internist has become physically or mentally incapacitated, regardless of cause and regardless of whether or not there has been an adjudication of incompetence, mental illness, or need for a committee, conservator, guardian, or other personal representative.

5. Successor Trustee When Grantor Disabled. Where Grantor is disabled, the next person selected from the provision below Additional or Successor Trustee shall serve as Cotrustee in place of Grantor. [Note: This is one of the most important decisions. Who should be in charge of your trust when you cannot serve as trustee or cotrustee?].

6. Grantor's Recovery from Disability. The Grantor shall be deemed to have recovered from any such disability when the other then serving Trustee receives written certification from Two (2) physicians regularly attending the Grantor, at least One (1) of which physicians is board certified in the specialty most closely associated with the alleged disability, that the Grantor is no longer physically or mentally incapacitated, and that Grantor is again able to manage his or her own financial affairs. The Trustee shall not be liable to any person, including Grantor, for the removal of the Grantor as a Trustee, if he or she acted in good faith on the certificates obtained in accordance with this provision. Upon such recovery, Grantor shall serve as a Cotrustee with any trustee theretofore serving. [Note: This is a commonly used provision but may not apply in the context of your situation as once your cognitive ability has declined to the point where you are not able to serve as a Cotrustee, this provision will never apply. In the event your illness is marked by intermittent attacks or exacerbations, this cumbersome process of declaring you "disabled" and then "recovered" makes little sense to repeat].

2. Charitable Bequest Following Grantor's Death. The Trustee shall distribute an amount equal to AMOUNT Dollars ($*.00) to CHARITY NAME from the Trust Estate following the death of Grantor. The Trustee shall have the power and discretion to fund this gift wholly or partly in cash or kind, and to select the assets which shall constitute this gift. However, the Trustee shall determine the value all assets so selected, and assets comprising the Trust Estate. [Note: Give consideration to making some gift to the charity that is devoted to serving those with the illness you have and funding research to cure that disease. Even a small gift will enlarge the roster of those making such commitments and may thereby enhance overall fund-raising efforts, even current fund-raising].

3. Grantor's Investment Goals for Trust Estate.
　　a. Grantor hereby communicates Grantor's general investment goals to the Trustee. Grantor states that *DESCRIBE INVESTMENT POLICY. [Note: See Chapter 12 for a discussion of investment planning for you in light of your chronic illness. Your investment goals may differ from those of someone without your health considerations. But it is impossible without further details and planning to understand how it should differ. If you establish a living trust your financial adviser should help you address this].
　　b. In formulating any investment policy or making any decision with respect to any assets, and assets relating to any closely held or family business and investment interests, it is Grantor's direction and intent that such interests may be held in the reasonable judgment of the Trustee. [Note: If you have a business you want retained, it should be addressed].
　　c. Grantor expressly directs the Trustee endeavor to retain Grantor's personal residence located at HOME ADDRESS if feasible for Grantor to remain there. Grantor does not make this an absolute prohibition against sale in light of the possibility that Grantor may benefit from residing in an assisted living or other facility. Grantor recommends that the Trustee consider Grantor's strong desire, but not mandate, that Grantor remain in said home, the modifications previously made to the home to accommodate Grantor and an future aide or companion, and other factors.
　　d. Grantor expressly authorizes, as an exception to the Prudent Investor Act, the Trustees to invest a portion of the trust estate in gift annuities provided through the auspices of CHARITY NAME even if these gift annuities are not an optimal or advisable investment allocation. Grantor authorizes the Trustees to consider Grantor's personal goals of benefit such charity in its research efforts to find a cure for CHRONIC DISEASE and other efforts through the use of gift annuities. [Note: Gift annuities can be an important source of fund-raising for many of the charities devoted to combating various chronic illnesses. However, a trustee may be precluded from purchasing such annuities by the Prudent Investor Act, a law which directs how trustees should invest trust assets. If you wish to permit this a specific exception to protect and direct the trustees may be necessary].

4. Trustee Decision Making and Authority.
　　a. Any authority, discretion or power granted to or conferred upon the Cotrustees by this Trust may be exercised by any such Trustees who shall be acting under this Trust Agreement at such time, or by such one of them who shall be so designated by an instrument in writing executed by any other Trustee.
　　b. Any one of the Cotrustees acting alone and without any requirement for joint action is authorized and permitted to complete alone any ministerial and administrative act, including but not limited to routine banking, investment, and brokerage transactions, except that when an institutional trustee is serving as a Cotrustee hereunder only such Institutional Cotrustee shall make investment decisions. It is the express intent of this provision to permit the Grantor when not disabled to continue to manage routine matters within the Grantor's purview, and to permit the Cotrustee other than the Grantor to manage routine matters when the Grantor is subject to an Ignored Disability.
　　c. This paragraph, however, shall not be interpreted or applied in a manner that violates any restriction in the provisions governing an Independent Trustee, person under legal obligation. Therefore, where the provisions governing an Independent Trustee apply, the Independent Trustee alone may make any such decisions or take any actions reasonably within the purview of such Independent Trustee.
　　d. Where there are more than Two (2) Trustees at any time the decision of a majority of them shall control and shall be binding on all of the Trustees.

e. If Two (2) or more Trustees are acting hereunder, the following provisions shall apply where the context permits:

i. The corporate or institutional Trustee shall have custody of the Trust Estate and of the books and records of the Trust.

ii. With respect to any matter as to which the Trustees have joint authority, a Trustee from time to time may delegate any or all of that Trustee's rights, powers, duties, and discretion as Trustee to the other Trustee, with the consent of the latter.

iii. The Trustee may establish bank accounts and it shall be assumed unless specified otherwise in the application for such account that checks or drafts may be drawn on, or withdrawals made from, any such account on the individual signature of either Trustee.

iv. A Trustee shall be presumed to have approved a proposed act or decision to refrain from acting if that Trustee fails to indicate approval or disapproval therefore within Thirty (30) days after written Notice requesting approval.

CHAPTER 11

CHARITABLE GIVING

INTRODUCTION TO CHARITABLE GIVING AND YOUR ESTATE PLAN

PEOPLE CONTRIBUTE TO CHARITY primarily for personal reasons. Usually those personal reasons are to help a cause and goal they are concerned about, for example, promoting research to rid the world of a chronic illness, like the one you're battling now. But charitable giving can also be tailored to help specific needs for you or your family. When helping a particular person along with benefiting a cause important to you are combined, the personal gratification and benefits of charitable giving can outweigh the tax and financial rewards. When you, or a family member or loved one, suffers from a chronic illness, commonly used charitable giving techniques can be tailored to address your needs, or the needs of that specific person. It does not require new-fangled charitable giving techniques, just molding traditional charitable planning to personal circumstances. This requires an understanding of the particular chronic illness involved, and the tax and charitable giving techniques available.

If you have a chronic illness, you may feel powerless. Structuring a charitable gift, even if it doesn't make an immediate difference for you or your loved one, will give you the feeling that you are making a difference. This can empower you and make you feel that you are doing something constructive to combat the illness affecting you. Typically, a parent's or sibling's first reaction to your diagnosis is to ask how they can help. Suggest a donation.

DONATE APPRECIATED STOCKS FOR GIFT ANNUITIES

This is a common staple of charitable planning. But while many donors will simply donate securities with no benefit other than a charitable deduction, for someone living with a chronic illness, this may not be enough. For people in this situation, cash flow for living expenses and medical costs are vital. If you sell appreciated securities, you will pay a capital gains tax. You will then have to invest and manage the proceeds, which may not be practical for you as your chronic illness progresses. If instead, you donate appreciated securities to a charity in exchange for a gift annuity, this will provide you with a charitable contribution deduction (which will vary based on age) and cash flow in the form of an annuity for the rest of your life. This not only provides an income tax benefit but also eliminates the need for you to continue to manage the assets. Your investment and cash flow are on autopilot. If you're struggling with other demands and stress related to a particular chronic illness, having a portion of your portfolio converted to a tax-advantaged annuity might be appropriate. But unlike a mere commercial annuity, a gift annuity with a charitable organization funding research to find a cure for your illness provides an important additional benefit. But you should be careful about how much you can commit to gift annuities (or charitable remainder trusts, CRTs) because once the gift/donation is made, you cannot access the principal in the event of an emergency.

FAMILY MEMBERS CAN USE INSURANCE TO BENEFIT YOU AND A CHARITY

A healthy spouse or family member can often use life insurance planning to benefit both you and a charity that can help your goals.

EXAMPLE

Janice Gordon has two daughters and a son, Phillip, who has multiple sclerosis. Janice is adamant that her will bequeath assets equally as she does not want to create any animosity or jealously amongst the children. Janice is especially concerned about keeping the peace because her daughters have been wonderfully supportive and helpful of her son. However, Janice realistically understands that Phillip cannot work more than a limited amount, and that although his training as a CPA would have provided him a good living, the fatigue and cognitive problems caused by his multiple sclerosis have undermined his ability to maintain what Janice believes is an adequate lifestyle. Janice's will simply leaves all assets to her children equally. Janice establishes an irrevocable (cannot be changed) life insurance trust that purchases a $2 million universal insurance policy on her life. This trust is designed to help support and supplement Phillip. If Phillip marries and has children, on Phillip's death, the funds in the trust will be distributed to his children. Janice feels this is important because Phillip does not have the capacity to earn enough to support his children and cannot easily obtain life insurance because of his multiple sclerosis. If Phillip dies without children, the National Multiple Sclerosis Society is named as the beneficiary of the remaining insurance proceeds. Janice is grateful for all the assistance that the National Multiple Sclerosis Society has provided to her son and believes that would be a good way to acknowledge the organization and also help others with the same struggle as Phillip.

IMPLEMENT A REVOCABLE LIVING TRUST WITH A CHARITABLE REMAINDER

For anyone suffering with a chronic illness such as Alzheimer's, ALS, or Huntington's disease, establishing a revocable living trust to manage assets as the disease leads to significant disability is an important estate, financial, and personal planning step. If you establish a revocable trust to provide for the management of your assets, consider permitting some amount of charitable donations by the trustees, including the possible purchase of gift annuities from designated charities devoted to helping those with your chronic illness. This is important because if contributions and even gift annuities aren't addressed specifically, the trustee may be precluded from taking these steps, or may be so concerned about violating his fiduciary duties as trustee that he might refrain from doing so even if not absolutely prohibited by law.

CRT TO BENEFIT YOURSELF

If you're a business owner, and it is getting more difficult for you to manage the business as your chronic disease progresses, an exit strategy will eventually become necessary. You could donate the business to a charitable remainder trust (CRT), which could then sell the business without your incurring a capital gains tax. The proceeds can be reinvested and the CRT would pay you a periodic annuity for life. This annuity could cover a significant portion of your medical and living expenses. On your death, the money remaining in the CRT will be given to the charity you've selected, or to a surviving spouse if you wish, and thereafter to the charity. This is a traditional application of a CRT technique to accomplish a number of your estate and financial planning goals. The timing of the sale could be based on the progression of your chronic illness, not market forces for maximizing return. The charity you select could be one whose mission is to further research or provide assistance for those with the chronic illness you are living with. The benefits of this application of a CRT will be substantial.

EXAMPLE

Adam wants to provide for the protection of his wife Dana who suffers from Parkinson's. Adam contemplates donating $1 million of stock that he has held for many years and which has appreciated substantially over its $150,000 purchase price. Adam has already engaged in considerable estate planning to benefit his and Dana's children and feels that is important to support the National Parkinson Foundation following his and Dana's deaths. Adam is hopeful that setting up a CRT for the National Parkinson Foundation will encourage others to make major current and deferred gifts, thereby hastening the research that will hopefully help is wife. Adam decides to establish an inter vivos (while he is alive) charitable remainder trust (CRT) for both himself and Dana. Both Adam and Dana will have current interests in the CRT. A current income tax deduction will be permitted, based on the present value of the future interest the National Parkinson Foundation will receive. A deduction is permitted because the rights of the National Parkinson Foundation are fixed in a manner that conforms to the tax law requirements for a current deduction. A specified payout must occur in each year (or more frequent period if required in the trust). No additional payments may be made to Adam or Dana, other than those fixed in the CRT document when it is established. Properly structured, this will also qualify for a gift tax marital deduction (because Adam is making a gift to Dana through the annuity payments she will receive during her lifetime). However, should Dana face an emergency, the trustees cannot distribute principal of the trust to her, so Adam has made sure there are other resources for her in the event of an emergency. After the death of both Adam and Dana, the principal remaining in the trust is to be distributed to the National Parkinson Foundation to establish a research grant in their memory. The National Parkinson Foundation is the remainder beneficiary of the CRT.

MARITAL GIFT FOLLOWED BY SPOUSAL CRT

If your spouse is living with a chronic illness, you can gift appreciated assets, such as growth stock mutual funds, to your spouse. Your spouse can then establish a CRT for his or her benefit, and contribute the appreciated mutual funds to the CRT. The CRT can continue the current investments as long as necessary. At the appropriate time, the mutual funds can be sold and the proceeds reinvested (free of any capital gains tax) in income oriented funds. The income from the CRT's revised asset allocation strategy can be used to pay your spouse an annuity for life. Your spouse won't have to address management of the assets, provided he or she uses the services of a trustee. An income tax charitable contribution deduction could be realized on your joint income tax return when the CRT is initially formed and the mutual funds contributed. Your spouse can have an annuity payment made monthly or quarterly for the rest of his or her life. After your spouse dies, the designated charity will receive the remaining assets held in the CRT. But the charity will realize intangible benefits from the date the CRT is initially formed in that it will be able to reflect the commitment in its efforts to solicit other donors. This can boost fund-raising efforts for the charity, something likely to be of significant importance to you. This approach may also be used to maximize the distributions to your spouse. If the chronically ill spouse has multiple sclerosis, for example, her lifespan may not be adversely affected so that the support of the CRT will be needed for a substantial time period. In such instances, a unitrust that can provide more inflation protection may be warranted. In a unitrust, a percentage of the fair value of the trust assets each year is used to determine the annuity payment (instead of a fixed percentage of the initial trust assets determining the annuity). If the value of the assets increases over time, the value of the annuity will as well. The theory is that this increase will help the annuity maintain its purchasing power even in the face of inflation.

If your spouse has a chronic illness, establishing a trust for his or her benefit can be an important planning step because there is no guarantee that you can care for this person indefinitely. While it is often assumed that spouse with the chronic illness will die first, the caregiver often succumbs first because of the stress of caregiving. Caregiving for a spouse with ALS, Parkinson's, or another chronic illness who has difficulty getting out of bed, getting down the stairs, etc., can be very difficult. Often, it involves physically moving the disabled spouse, which can be very stressful to the caregiver, especially if he or she is elderly. When such physical support is prolonged, the physical consequences for the caregiver can be debilitating and even deadly.

EXAMPLE

Cindy's husband Sam has ALS. Cindy wants to provide financial protection and management (in the event something happens to her) for Sam for his life, but on his demise, Cindy wants to benefit the ALS Association. Cindy establishes an inter vivos (while she is alive) marital trust (QTIP) for him, Sam. Sam has a current interest in the trust. No current income tax deduction is permitted for the future interest the charity will receive after Sam's death. No deduction is permitted because the rights of the ALS Association as the charity are not fixed in a manner that conforms to the tax law requirements for a current deduction. To protect Sam, the trust may pay any necessary amounts of the trust principal (assets) to Sam, or for his benefit, during Sam's lifetime. A trust company is named as sole trustee. This assures that since Sam can no longer fully participate in the management of the trust, a bank will provide for whatever financial and other services he needs. Properly structured, this trust will qualify for a gift tax marital deduction when Cindy establishes it. During Sam's lifetime, all income must be distributed at least annually to him or for his benefit. In addition, should Sam face an emergency, the trustees could distribute principal for the benefit of Sam as they see fit. On Sam's demise, the principal remaining in the trust is to be distributed to the ALS Society, the remainder beneficiary. There will not be any current charitable contribution deduction. However, on Sam's death, although the value of the entire trust will be included in his taxable estate, there will be an equal and offsetting charitable contribution deduction. This approach ensures flexibility in case Sam lives for longer than the typical person with ALS.

CLT TO BENEFIT TARGET CHARITY AND CHILD WITH CHRONIC ILLNESS

A charitable lead trust (CLT) is a trust designed to benefit a charity and at the same time provide a future gift (inheritance) to your child (or other heir) at a substantially reduced gift tax cost. When you establish a CLT, the designated charity receives an annuity payment (the greater the percentage payment, the more substantial the tax benefit), for the number of years you specify (the greater the number of years, the greater the tax benefit). Thereafter, the assets in the trust will be distributed to the child (or other heir you named). This approach can be a tremendous way to help fund research to find a cure for the illness your child or other heir is living with while ensuring a safety net for the child's financial future. It's also a great way for you to feel that you are fighting your child's disease proactively.

This approach may be viable for some chronic illnesses, but not for others. For example, a child with relapsing-remitting MS may have a relatively long career span expectancy. In this case, a charitable lead trust could be used over a long enough period to minimize gift taxes, benefit a charity conducting MS research, and provide a financial safety net for the child. MS is typically diagnosed when a patient is in his or her twenties to fifties, which, depending on the type of MS, may permit this type of long term CLT planning. The same may be true of a other chronic illnesses such as Crohn's disease patients, who can lead a relatively long life. However, this approach may not be viable for a person diagnosed with Parkinson's or Alzheimer's disease. These latter diseases, with the exception of their young-onset versions, are typically found in older people. Huntington's disease is a degenerative brain disorder that undermines an individual's ability to think, walk, and speak. Eventually, a person with Huntington's disease becomes totally dependent upon others for care. The time span between initial diagnosis to the development of significant disability may be as short as five to ten years. If a CLT were used for a child with Huntington's disease, the remainder interest should be paid to a trust for the child's benefit as independent management may be essential.

CHARITABLE BAILOUT OF A CLOSELY HELD BUSINESS TO BENEFIT HEIRS

Donations to the Michael J. Fox Foundation, Inc. (MJFF), or a charitable remainder trust to benefit MJFF, can have special use when a key asset is stock in a closely held business. A charitable bailout of a closely held business' stock can address important planning problems for a closely held business owner. Stock in a closely held corporation can be difficult, or impossible, to sell. This is because any outsider will generally be very reluctant to own a minority interest in a close corporation. Another potential problem relates to the type of corporation involved. Assume that the corporation is a C corporation (i.e., not an S corporation) and has available cash that you would like to donate to the MJFF. However, it may not be practical to make a dividend distribution to provide the cash for such a donation because a dividend distribution will result in double taxation. Another common problem scenario for a closely held business is when a parent owns stock in a close corporation and wishes to transfer control to a child without triggering income tax on redemption. One possible solution for this latter scenario is called a stock bailout. Under the terms of a stock bailout, you can make a gift of any portion of the stock in your corporation to the MJFF. At some later date, the charity may, in its sole discretion, sell some of the stock back to your corporation. This could provide you with a charitable contribution deduction for the value of the stock donated. The MJFF can eventually receive a cash amount for the contribution. When the corporation redeems the stock, the interest of the children owning stock will increase. This is because the charitable bailout/redemption of your stock will increase their relative ownership interest. As your illness progresses, this technique could be a useful part of your exit strategy from your business.

OTHER CHARITABLE PLANNING TIPS

When you or a loved one plans a charitable gift, consider the pitfalls and problems that these gifts can raise with your accountant and financial planner. The list below is not all-inclusive and barely touches upon the complexity. The take home message is that many charitable planning transactions have complex tax and other twists that are best dealt with by a professional.

Loss Property

Do not donate assets that have declined in value. Consider transferring or selling the loss property (e.g., a rental property you purchased for $300,000 that is now worth only $200,000) now to take advantage of the losses, or gift the loss property to a spouse who may be able to take advantage of it later. Be sure not to use this for funding charitable gifts since the loss in the asset won't be realized. If you sell the property at a loss and donate the proceeds to charity, you may get some tax benefits from the loss.

Testamentary Bequests

Another common trap is the manner in which a testamentary bequest is structured. Too often a bequest is assumed to be simple, when in fact, a host of complex issues can be raised.

EXAMPLE

Jim Fitzgerald has two adult children, a son, Thomas, and a daughter, Sandy, who is in her thirties and has secondary-progressive MS. While Jim would prefer to leave assets equally to his two children on his death, he is not certain this is fair, given the uncertainty about the progression of Sandy's MS. Some of the new grading systems being developed leave Jim cautiously optimistic that Sandy's MS won't progress to a level that will require him to distribute his estate unequally. After reviewing the matter with the family, Jim opts for the following dispositive scheme in his will: 55 percent to Sandy, 40 percent to Thomas, and 5 percent to the Department of Neurosciences at the University of Medicine and Dentistry of New Jersey (UMDNJ).

When Jim discusses this plan with his attorney, a couple of important issues are raised. While there is a likelihood that Sandy will need more financial assistance than Thomas, that really cannot be known for certain: The progression of her disease is unknown, and there are new therapies being developed. Just as importantly, Jim's attorney points out that there is no certainty that Thomas will not face some type of financial, health, or other adversity. Finally, Jim's attorney explains that if a percentage of his estate is left to charity, the will and financial reporting will have to be submitted to the state's attorney general's office to comply with state law. The attorney further points out the valuation issues that can arise if a percentage of an estate is left to charity. Jim anticipates that the family vacation home in the country will be kept by both Thomas and Sandy, for personal use for them and their children. For estate tax purposes, the children have the incentive to value this house as low as possible to minimize estate tax costs. However, the UMDNJ, as an independent charitable beneficiary, is obligated to ensure that fair market values are used. The greater the value of the vacation home the greater the charity's 5 percent interest. This disparity in goals could create some friction. The combination of these and other issues, the attorney explains, makes a donation of a percentage of the estate potentially problematic. So Jim settles on the following dispositive scheme: A fixed dollar bequest of $500,000 in his will to the UMDNJ to be used to develop programming and facilities in the chapter in which Sandy has been active. The remaining estate is divided three ways: 40 percent to Thomas and 40 percent to Sandy, with each bequest to be structured in a separate trust designed to meet the specific needs of each child. The remaining 20 percent of the estate is to be distributed to a family "pot" trust, which can benefit any child or grandchild based on need. The family trust will likely be divided into two components: GST exempt and non-exempt. The children and the charity all benefit from this revised plan.

Select IRD Assets for Charitable Gifts

If you have a chronic illness, consider the types of assets you own. To the extent that you have accounts receivable, individual retirement accounts (IRAs), or other assets that are subject to income taxation under the income in respect of a decedent rules (IRD), you may want to consider bequeathing these assets to a charity because the charity won't have to recognize the income tax, and you will get a reduction in estate values. These are the most advantageous assets to use.

LEGAL CONSTRAINTS ON CHARITABLE GIVING

Consider revising durable powers of attorney to expressly permit your agents to make gifts to a charity or a particular cause. Similarly, if you own interests in LLCs or corporations that you might wish to donate, be certain while you are able to negotiate and implement a change, that the entity's governing documents are modified to remove restrictions on charitable transfers, or to at least permit them with certain conditions.

CHAPTER SUMMARY

You don't have to be a millionaire to make a donation that has an impact on a charitable cause important to you. As this chapter suggests, many people living with chronic illness have long lives and successful careers, and good charitable planning can enable others to give. Giving (to any degree and in any amount) to charities fighting chronic illness can accomplish a host of important goals and should be part of every estate and financial plan.

CHAPTER 12

OTHER CONSIDERATIONS

PLANNING FOR FAMILY MEMBERS

IF YOU HAVE A CHRONIC ILLNESS, your situation should be considered in light of the estate and financial planning of your family members. This discussion provides an overview of some of the points to evaluate.

SHOULD YOU RESIGN AS AGENT AND FIDUCIARY UNDER FAMILY DOCUMENTS?

If you were recently diagnosed with a chronic illness that will affect your ability to manage your finances and affairs, you owe it to your loved ones to consider the appropriateness of resigning as an agent, trustee, or executor under their estate planning documents. Doing so while you are competent and able to execute the documents releasing you from serving as agent, trustee, or executor is simpler and easier than having others address this situation later.

EXAMPLE

Uncle Joe, now age 85, has always trusted and relied upon you and named you as agent under his power of attorney to help him out. You were recently diagnosed with ALS. The prudent step would be to advise Uncle Joe to have his attorney revise his power of attorney and name a different agent.

HOW YOUR CHRONIC ILLNESS AFFECTS YOUR SPOUSE/PARTNER'S OR PARENT'S WILLS

Your chronic illness may have an important effect on how your spouse, partner, parent, or other family members' wills should be prepared if they are naming you a beneficiary. There are a few things they should to take into consideration in their planning as it pertains to you. Unless you are substantially well off, it may be advisable given the often draining financial cost of medical treatment and the possibility of long term health care costs, for your family to leave any bequests to you in the form of a Special Needs Trust (SNT). An SNT can be set up to provide you with benefits only in excess of what state and other governmental benefits won't cover. These extra or special need payment restrictions should safeguard these inherited assets from undermining your qualification for vital government programs. It should also safeguard these inherited assets for your use.

Regardless of your financial position, loved ones considering bequeathing you money should tailor trusts to hold the assets they leave you. Those trusts should not consist of the boilerplate trust provisions incorporating the many misconceptions about planning for chronic illness. Instead, they should follow the planning decisions and structure you've determined, based on a review of this book and meeting with your estate planner. If possible, you should be a cotrustee of the trust established for your benefit. Special precautions may have to be taken if an incremental goal is to prevent those assets from being taxed in your estate. For example, your family member's estate planner may limit your right as a cotrustee to withdraw money from the trust solely to maintain your standard of living (an "ascertainable standard" in tax jargon) and take other steps. Since these are complex tax matters, your family member's advisers will need to address them. They are beyond the scope of this book.

KEY

> In many situations, depending on which chronic illness you have and the extent to which it currently affects you, there is no reason for you not to be a cotrustee and be actively involved in a trust a family member sets up for you.

PLANNING FOR YOUR PARTNER/SPOUSE

If you are married or have a partner, planning for chronic illness should also include special consideration for the role that a partner or spouse fulfills as caregiver. Caregiving requires time and emotional capital, and can take a substantial toll on the caregiver. Studies have reported that about one-third of caregivers have high blood pressure, about one-third have high cholesterol, about 15 percent suffer from chronic headaches, about 15 percent have persistent sleep disorders, and nearly one-fifth have mood disorders. These facts need to be kept in mind when discussing basic estate planning decisions. For example, when evaluating whom to name as trustee of your revocable living trust, consider naming an institutional cotrustee (or other cotrustee) to ease the administrative burden on your caregiver. Too often those planning for someone with a chronic illness focus only on the person living with the illness, with no regard for the impact that illness has on loved ones and caregivers. This also supports a more aggressive recommendation for you to name an institutional cofiduciary whenever practicable.

Partners or spouses should also revise their estate planning documents to ensure that any assets left to you are left in a trust to provide for a management structure as discussed above. In some situations a special needs trust may be advisable.

RELIGIOUS CONSIDERATIONS

Few lawyers address religion in their legal documents. However, when dealing with the life and death decisions discussed in Chapter 7 on living wills and health care proxies, charitable giving discussed in Chapter 11, and a host of other issues mentioned in this book, religious considerations are important for many people. Many turn to their religious faith in the face of adversity. Because you are living with a chronic disease, you may well find solace in your religious roots. Even if you have not, perhaps your loved ones have. In either case, you might wish to address religious considerations with your attorney. There are many provisions, documents, and planning steps that might warrant modification to address religious concerns, and some are discussed below. It is not a comprehensive listing, but a sampling of issues and situations that you might wish to discuss with a religious adviser as well as with your estate planning professionals.

SELECTING FIDUCIARIES

If you are seeking to imbue your estate planning documents with religious values or to transmit a particular religious heritage to a child or other heir, one of the most important decisions you can make is to select fiduciaries that have one or all of the following: knowledge of the particular faith, affiliation or observance of that faith themselves, and/or sensitivity to the specific needs of the heirs in light of the religious goals and objectives. In many instances, the person that best fits these criteria will not be the person best suited to handle investment and other fiduciaries responsibilities. Your selection of fiduciaries will have a profound impact on your ability to transmit values. The context of fiduciaries should not only include trustees, but also agents under a power of attorney in the event a chronic illness or other incapacity results in the power being the operative document for many years.

DISTRIBUTIONS

The agents (under your power of attorney) and fiduciaries (executors and trustees under your will) should be given guidance and granted legal authority to disburse funds for religious education (e.g., supplemental religious education or private school), religious travel (pilgrimages to holy sites), charitable giving (to inculcate a core religious value in heirs), and other purposes consistent with your religious goals. Boilerplate distribution provisions in many documents just won't suffice.

CHARITABLE GIVING

Every religion advocates the virtues of charity, but charitable giving can be tailored to reflect the unique nuances of your faith. While many religions mandate tithing a certain percentage of income or assets to charity, others provide more specific standards. For example, charitable giving is an essential part of the Baha'i faith as it demonstrates devotion to Baha'Allah and represents the ideal of charity. Baha'is are expected to give a certain percentage of their income and assets to Baha'i charitable organizations through a mandatory donation referred to as "Huququ'llah" (The Right of God).

HEROIC MEASURES

Perhaps the single phrase in all of estate planning that has more potential religious repercussions than any other is the mandate in a living will or health care proxy that "no heroic measures" be taken. There are, apart from the obvious ambiguities of this phrase, a host of moral and ethical considerations that anyone with religious sensitivity needs to address. Some people, depending on their religious convictions or upbringing, assume that they can never withdraw life support without violating their religious standards. Often, this interpretation is incorrect, but the issue is complex and often fraught with religious nuance that cannot easily be resolved. For example, the Catholic Church does not mandate that a person be kept alive no matter what. A Catholic can decide to avoid overly invasive and experimental procedures, but not ordinary means of care. "Ordinary means" could include feeding someone, making certain they have air to breathe, etc. According to the Catholic Church, then, a patient must continue to receive ordinary care; otherwise, those denying that care are effectively acting to cause the patient's death. The extraordinary means go beyond this and seek to reverse a process that is already underway. Extraordinary means can be antibiotics or surgery, among others. For a Hindu, the perspective may be that one lives as long as one naturally can, and then accepts the end as and when it happens. If a person has suffered severe brain damage and there is no hope of recovery, there is no basis for prolonging life by artificial means under Hindu principles.

EXAMPLE

Many religious faiths take issue with terminating life support based on a lack of quality of life. The view taken by some is that life in any form is sacred and must be preserved. If you have Alzheimer's disease, the prognosis is dementia. This may or may not make the quality of life issue relevant to you, your family, or your designated agents. If it is, it should be addressed directly and explicitly in your documents. This issue is particularly important within the context of provision of nutrition and hydration. Should nutrition and hydration be provided to you if you have advanced dementia and are unaware of your surroundings?

PREGNANCY AND MEDICAL DECISIONS

Every woman should carefully address the issues of pregnancy in her living will and/or health proxy because medical decision-making concerning a mother and her fetus varies greatly among different religions. Generally Catholicism proscribes taking direct action that would cause the death of an unborn child or the mother. You cannot choose the life of the mother over the life of the unborn child, or vice versa, since all life is sacred and that decision lies in God's hands alone. Unless this matter is expressly addressed in your living will, no one may know the degree of your devotion. You cannot expect health care providers to have the knowledge necessary to carry out your wishes without clear guidance from you. In contrast, under Jewish and Islamic law, saving the mother's life is generally given preference to saving the life of a fetus. If your illness may affect your pregnancy, you should discuss the possible additional risks and complications with your physician and, if appropriate, modify the provisions of your living will accordingly.

PAIN RELIEF

Many patients and health care providers view the alleviation of all pain to be an essential and ideal objective. The nature of your chronic illness may have a profound impact on how you view this, but different religions view the concept of pain differently. For an Orthodox Christian, the act of suffering can mean purification, redemption, and salvation. While suffering is clearly not encouraged, pain relief that renders people unconscious during their last days may prevent them from partaking in profound and moving observances essential to their religious beliefs. The Christian Orthodox Church encourages you to be lucid during your last days so that you may confess sins and receive Holy Communion. If the attending physicians are not aware of this, they cannot be assumed to respect and foster this type of care. Similarly, according to Buddhist tradition, your consciousness near death directly correlates to the level of rebirth. Excessive pain relief could undermine this. However, Buddhists also believe that suffering is the converse of the optimal state of being. A sensitive balancing of important religious goals, and your wishes in light of your current and future health status, is thus required.

FUNERAL AND OTHER POST-DEATH ARRANGEMENTS

Most religions provide for specific post-death rituals. Under Jewish law, autopsies and embalming are generally prohibited. In Buddhist tradition, it is a common belief that incense should be burned near a person close to death, to guide your last thoughts upward toward enlightenment. Some Buddhists believe that for a period following death, for a minimum of at least one week, the spirit may remain with the body and the body should therefore not be moved. Because these traditions may be impossible to carry out in almost any American medical or health care facility, people who wish to meet death according to these rites and rituals should consider making advance arrangements to spend their last days in a hospice sensitive to these religious beliefs or at home. Some religions prohibit cremation, other religions or cultures favor it. These issues can be addressed in your living will, health proxy, and in some instances in your will (if, for example, you choose to be buried in another country or under other circumstances which create considerable cost).

DISPOSITION OF ASSETS ON DEATH

A secular will may have to be modified to reflect the Baha'i, Jewish, Islamic, or other religious laws of inheritance. The Quran and Old Testament include detailed provisions as to how inheritance must be handled. While some of these provisions are similar, they are typically addressed quite differently in will drafting and should, in any case, be coordinated with tax, estate, financial and succession planning, and ethical issues. For the Christian Orthodox, not providing for family and relatives is tantamount to disowning your faith. For Catholics, there are general but vital guidelines regarding charity and justice.

DISPUTE RESOLUTION

For all faiths, disputes of a religious or spiritual nature are perhaps best resolved through mandatory arbitration before a designated religious body, not a secular court. Both Buddhism and the Baha'i faith incorporate principles that affect how disputes should be addressed. The disinheritance of an heir and the use of in-terrorem clauses need to be evaluated. The Buddhist theory of Karma provides that everything done in a particular life, as well as in past lives, influences and affects future lives. If you disinherit an heir out of anger, it can be viewed as creating a negative influence that may be carried on through rebirth to the next life. Buddhism advocates that you take action out of compassion and not anger.

INVESTMENT STANDARDS

The Prudent Investor Act and the investment provisions of the governing document should be tailored to permit a religious or socially oriented investment strategy if that strategy meets your religious or other personal beliefs.

FINANCIAL PLANNING CONSIDERATIONS

Investment planning is an integral part of your estate and related planning. If your funds are not properly invested, your estate could be dissipated before you die rendering all your careful planning and tailored documents useless. Just as with many of the estate planning documents and techniques discussed above, many investment advisers and financial planners operate under misconceptions and apply incorrect generalizations about investment planning for those with chronic illness.

The symptoms that commonly accompany many chronic illnesses can make it difficult to manage assets. Consolidation and simplification of investments and other assets is advisable. This approach will provide you with a greater ability to control resources even if physical or cognitive impairments make record keeping more difficult. Comprehensive financial planning should be undertaken to ensure that your resources will not run out. Such planning should consider and address:

❖ A reduction in work time and hence salary, or cessation of work altogether.

❖ Possible shortened career duration.

❖ Your receipt of money from an existing disability insurance policy purchased prior to your diagnosis.

❖ Near and long-term effects on the earnings of a caregiver partner/spouse.

❖ Costly medications, if insurance now or in the future may not cover them.

❖ Modifications to make to your home to accommodate your disability.

In light of these and other factors you should reevaluate your investment risk tolerance, return needs, and resulting investment allocation. With new uncertainties and costs, you may need to reduce the previous accepted level of investment risk. On the other hand, your budget projections might demonstrate that the new financial reality requires greater investment risks to meet new needs and goals.

These decisions could also have an impact on the investment provisions in your will and trusts. Prior to diagnosis, your documents may have included broad investment clauses permitting holding non-liquid, non-diversified assets, closely held business interests and so forth, all without regard to Prudent Investor Act limitations. These may now warrant revision to meet the mandates of the Prudent Investor Act, and may include risk-return analysis and maintaining a diversified portfolio that considers all relevant factors. In very simple terms, the Prudent Investor Act mandates that funds be invested in as diversified manner to reduce risk and maximize return.

BUSTING INVESTING MYTHS

The knee-jerk reactions of most wealth managers and estate planners to clients with chronic illness can be dangerously wrong.

❖ **Myth:** Investors with chronic illness need liquidity.

❖ **Reality:** Some do, many don't. You may actually have significant savings, an insurance safety net, and continued earnings from employment. Others will not. Making assumptions that planning is "standard" won't serve you well. While some people living with chronic illness prefer more liquidity in their investment portfolios than others, for many investors with chronic illness the opposite may be a sounder approach. If substantial liquidity is appropriate for you, the remainder of your investments may take on what is sometimes called a barbell investment strategy. More weight will be given to more aggressive equities to offset the low returns anticipated on the overweight allocation to cash. Bear in mind that this strategy may have higher volatility risk than alternative strategies.

❖ **Myth:** Clients with chronic illness should invest with a short-term time horizon.

❖ **Reality:** Some should, many shouldn't. Those with Alzheimer's disease generally survive about four to eight years after diagnosis, although some have survived much longer. Multiple sclerosis generally has no impact on longevity. Many clients with chronic illness need long-term investment planning, not short term. Even for people with a short life expectancy, the magnitude of their wealth and the nature of their estate plan may create long-term investment horizons for certain "buckets" of assets that will almost assuredly be bequeathed to heirs or spent. But there is significant variation, not only between different illnesses, but even among people living with the same illness. Focus on the real facts that pertain to your situation and make certain your advisers do the same.

❖ **Myth:** Clients with chronic illness need special needs trusts.

❖   **Reality:** Some chronic illnesses strike young people. However, others strike late in life. Thus, many people living with chronic illness have had a full work/career life and may have significant assets. For these individuals, a special needs arrangement (e.g., in a spouse's will) is not appropriate.

❖   **Myth:** Budget projections are standard.

❖   **Reality:** Some financial planners actually use the same canned investment and other assumptions for most of their clients, chronic illness or not. Others assume that all clients with chronic illness will live on government aid. Sometimes true, often not. Many elderly people diagnosed with chronic illnesses, for example, may have already acquired long-term care coverage. On the other hand, if your health insurance changes its coverage for your drug therapies, for example, your entire financial picture could be impacted if a previously modest monthly co-payment now triggers a $15,000 to $20,000 annual cost. What might the cost of modifying your home be? What about the cost of providing accommodations for a live-in caregiver? The "what-ifs" to budget properly are more complex and uncertain than for most people, and these issues need to be factored into the planning.

❖   **Myth:** If you face the uncertainties of a chronic illness, you cannot bear the same level of risk other investors would accept.

❖   **Reality:** Many chronically ill people have substantial wealth and can make the same risk/return decisions any other investor might choose. Many living with chronic illness could live for a decade or many decades. Structuring a portfolio with inadequate risk might leave you unprotected against the ravages of inflation, or worse, broke. In fact, some chronically ill investors may feel quite comfortable accepting a higher level of risk in order to meet long-term investment goals.

EXAMPLE

Jim is 28 years old and living with multiple sclerosis. He has a successful career but anticipates that he will have to retire by age 50 because of chronic fatigue and other symptoms. A possible asset allocation for Jim might be heavily weighted toward equities and alternative investments to create sufficient wealth to retire at 50, an allocation that might strike the typical 28-year-old as highly unusual. The disease may have given Jim sufficient financial maturity to realize that, if his work career has to extend another couple of years if the target is missed, the long-term plan would be challenging but still possible (e.g.. working with reduced hours, or out of a home-based office).

OTHER NUANCES OF WEALTH MANAGEMENT FOR THE CHRONICALLY ILL

Because you have a chronic illness, you need to view wealth management and estate planning differently from the way people without a chronic illness do. Some aspects of planning that your illness may have an effect on are discussed below:

❖ **Agent and fiduciary.** Your chronic illness creates a far greater likelihood of your investment advisers accepting investment and other direction from a fiduciary acting on your behalf. Set up a meeting early in the relationship with your planner so that you can be sure that she understands how your power of attorney, revocable trust, and other documents might affect your agents. Be certain that the decision-making authority and mechanisms your planner and other agents need to best serve you throughout your relationship are provided in the documents. Don't assume the documents will meet your needs. Have the adviser (or better yet, your adviser's attorney) review the provisions governing decision making, power and authority, investment allocation, etc. Make certain that your adviser has a copy of your power of attorney, and revocable living trust, if you have one.

❖ **Needs Analysis.** To properly budget and estimate future needs and services, consider having a consultation with your financial planner and a geriatric or similar consultant. An independent evaluation and report can better clarify your current and potential future circumstances and needs, which will help guide your wealth manager, estate planner, and other advisers.

❖ **Estate planning techniques.** Your investment planning must be coordinated with your estate planning. Don't let your adviser assume that you need not engage in estate tax minimization if in fact you have sufficient assets to warrant such planning. You must also inform your adviser how planning can proceed, but with a bias toward addressing your personal goals, such as retaining control over assets, and investment assets in particular, in light of the health uncertainties you face.

❖ **Annual meetings.** Annual meetings are strongly recommended.

Circumstances can change. Feelings will change. If you were recently diagnosed, it will take some time for you to come to terms with your illness and prognosis. As you gain a greater understanding of your condition, estate planning and personal and investment decisions will all evolve.

QUESTIONS TO DISCUSS WITH YOUR FINANCIAL PLANNER

There is a host of questions you should discuss with your financial planner. These will vary depending on your financial position, health, etc. Here are some suggestions:

❖   Are the types and limits of insurance coverage I have sufficient? Are they secure? Is there anything I should change?

❖   If there are gaps in my insurance coverage, what if anything can be done?

❖   How can I estimate possible large future expenses that should be reserved for?

❖   How can I analyze economically the net benefit of continuing to work? How long must I work to secure my financial future? How can I estimate the effect my illness will have on my earnings?

❖   Can you make the accommodations that I need for meetings to make it easier for me?

❖   How will my financial plan affect my estate and insurance planning?

❖   How frequently should we schedule review meetings?

❖   How can you help me determine the amount of risk I should, or must, tolerate in my investment plan in order to achieve my financial goals?

❖   How can we determine the minimum cash or liquidity that I need so that I can feel secure?

DEALING WITH HANDWRITING ISSUES

There are a number of chronic illnesses that result in symptoms that can make your handwriting difficult to read or illegible. Significantly, handwriting can vary depending on the course of your illness and may even depend on the time of day or the effect of your various medications.

Tremors can make writing difficult to read. Bradykinesia can make writing extremely slow. Micrographia results in letters getting smaller and smaller and closer and closer to each other. If you have more than one symptom, your signatures may change over the course of a long meeting. Several steps can be taken to address these issues:

❖　　Schedule extra time for signing meetings.

❖　　Large felt tip pens are often easier to manipulate than other writing utensils.

❖　　Use special or limited powers of attorney for executing documents at a business or other meeting. For example, if stock in a family business will be sold, to facilitate the closing have your attorney provide in the stock purchase (or other) agreement that you may be represented by an agent under a power of attorney at the closing and attach the proposed special power as an exhibit to the draft documents so that it can be approved in advance. Consider using a special power solely for the closing that grants your agent power to do all things necessary for the closing only and thereafter lapses. Be cognizant of the skepticism the IRS often shows toward estate planning transactions consummated under a power of attorney.

❖　　Create a special affidavit acknowledging the variations in your handwriting. This could be used to support the legitimate signing of documents even if writing is quite different. It may also be useful for you to have when signing documents at a bank or other location. The affidavit can include your name, address, and other identifying information, and then explain your chronic illness and the symptoms that affect your handwriting and how. The affidavit could be signed by you, witnessed, and notarized at different times to create a single history of the variation in your signature.

If signing documents is difficult and a power of attorney is utilized, consider having your attorney prepare a special power for purposes of having a named agent, and perhaps not a beneficiary of the plan, execute the documents to implement that one plan. In that special power of attorney document, your attorney may expressly state that the power is being executed to facilitate the execution of documents for that transaction solely because of the tremors or bradykinesia. If the transaction is challenged at a later date on the basis of competency, corroboration of competency and the specific power used for a specific physical purpose will differentiate that transaction from others.

WILL CHALLENGES AND OTHER LAWSUITS

Chronic illness is assumed by many to bring debilitation and incompetence. Regardless of the appropriateness of such assumptions to your situation, these generalizations and misconceptions make a challenge of your will (called a "will challenge") or of your other documents or planning, quite possible. The following two examples, each told from a different child's perspective, highlight the potential for challenges and lawsuits.

EXAMPLE 1: DAUGHTER'S PERSPECTIVE

Rebecca is 76 years old, lives in Connecticut, and has been diagnosed with AD. Rebecca has two children, Joan (the older) and Tom (the younger). Joan lives nearby and has helped her mother for years with household chores and bill paying. Tom lives in Nevada and is quite busy with his young family and career. There has always been jealousy between Joan and Tom. As Rebecca's situation has worsened, Joan gave up a promotion and substantial raise with her company because she felt it imperative to stay in Connecticut to help her mother. The relocation to Florida that the promotion would have required would have made caregiving impossible. Rebecca realized the sacrifices that Joan was making. In time, she decided to retitle several large accounts as joint accounts in both their names. After a fall and hip replacement surgery, it was hard for Rebecca to get around. She had Joan change these accounts using the power of attorney that the attorney prepared, naming Joan as agent. As Rebecca's AD progressed, she wasn't really competent to make decisions. Joan continued to care for her at the expense of her own career and social life. Since Rebecca had made it clear to Joan that she wanted her to inherit the joint accounts, Joan used other accounts to pay for Rebecca's expenses. By the time Rebecca died, the only assets left besides her home were the joint accounts with Joan. This was exactly what Rebecca wanted.

EXAMPLE 2: SON'S PERSPECTIVE

As Rebecca's situation has worsened, her daughter Joan, who never really pursued a career with any vigor, forced herself on her mother and began to control her and her finances. Rebecca realized the sacrifices that Tom had made to build his family and career and had always promised him help with his children's college costs. To prevent this from happening, after their mother already had lost substantial decision-making capacity, his sister Joan moved in for the kill. Joan, unbeknownst to her mother or brother, surreptitiously used a power of attorney to retitle several large accounts as joint accounts naming herself and her mother, so she would inherit them on her mother's death. As Rebecca's AD progressed, she really didn't have the competence to make decisions, so Joan used Rebecca's remaining accounts to pay for part-time caregiving with the intent of depleting any resources that Tom could inherit. Although Rebecca had made it clear to Tom that she wanted him to inherit extra funds to pay for his children's college, Joan used other accounts to pay for Rebecca's expenses. By the time Rebecca died, other than her home, the only assets left were the joint accounts with Joan. This was exactly the opposite of what Rebecca wanted.

Planning to document gifts, restricting gifts under powers of attorney, mandating equal gifts, coordinating title to assets, actions of agents under powers and dispositive provisions under wills and trusts, takes on greater importance if you have a chronic illness, and especially if that illness brings any cognitive dysfunction. Annual (or even more frequent) meetings with your advisers to monitor these matters and document your intent while you are able can be vital to securing your wishes. Steps that you might consider include:

❖   **Revise and re-sign your will.** If you have no or only limited cognitive impact and you are clearly competent, have your attorney add a few modifications to your prior will and supervise your re-signing the will with different witnesses from those who witnessed you signing your last will. Making a change demonstrates that you revisited and reconsidered your will. Re-signing with new witnesses and a different notary creates a pattern to demonstrate your intent in the event of a will challenge. If the most recent will is held invalid as a result of a challenge, the will signed some months earlier with nearly identical dispositive provisions will be reinstated.

❖   **Beneficiaries should not be present.** Be certain that the caregiver and anyone else receiving a bequest is not present when documents are signed and document this fact.

❖   **Document and explain unequal or unnatural bequests.** If the dispositive provision favors a particular heir, especially if that heir is the caregiver, explain and document in writing the reasoning for the disparate bequests. Have the caregiver/heir log his or her hours/efforts with an ongoing diary, and have an independent accountant estimate the economic cost (to the caregiver) of providing services.

❖   **Details.** List all family members' names and relationships in your will, and expressly name anyone to whom you are intentionally not making a bequest to avoid a challenge on the basis of the scrivener having left out that particular heir.

❖   **Prove competency.** Your attorney should take independent steps to corroborate your mental capacity at the time any document is signed.

Chapter Summary

Estate planning is not just about the obvious documents you need to sign. There are a number of ancillary issues that may be important to carrying out your wishes. Use your planners to identify the ones pertinent to you and what steps need to be taken on your behalf. If there are other issues important to you that are not mentioned, be vocal and tell your advisers about them.

CHAPTER 13

GETTING STARTED

HOW TO USE THIS BOOK AS A WORKBOOK TO PLAN YOUR ESTATE AND DOCUMENTS

Estate Planning for People with a Chronic Condition or Disability provides valuable tips and information on how to tailor your estate planning documents for your special considerations. Because many of the issues raised here concern complex matters, it is a good idea to discuss those that apply to your unique needs with your estate planning attorney. Address with your attorney all your wishes regarding your health care proxy, living will, HIPAA release, power of attorney, charitable planning, your will, and (if appropriate) a revocable living trust. Also talk with your attorney about the numerous ways your chronic disease may affect specific legal documents that should be prepared to safeguard you and those important to you. If hiring an attorney is not in your budget, you can use the sample forms in this book, forms found on www.laweasy.com, and forms that may be mandated by your state's statutes (laws).

Make lists of the points from this book that apply to you and explain (to yourself and your attorney) how you think the recommendations or suggested language in the documents contained in the appendixes of this book should be tailored or changed to fit your personal circumstances. If you feel that the forms presented here do not adequately address your needs, write your questions or comments in the margins and ask your estate planner to help you address any necessary modifications. Remember that your final documents should reflect all relevant issues that are of concern to you, today and in the future if the progression of your chronic illness indicates that change is likely to occur.

Whatever your decisions, give serious thought to supplementing the legal documents with a heartfelt letter that sets forth and elaborates on your feelings about all the issues relevant to your circumstances. Although such a letter is not legally binding, it can go a long way to guiding your loved ones in carrying out your wishes, especially if the time comes when you are no longer able to communicate those wishes.

HOW FORMS BECOME FINAL DOCUMENTS

The following forms are included in this book:

- ❖ Power of Attorney

- ❖ HIPAA Release

- ❖ Living Will

- ❖ Health Care Proxy (or Medical Power of Attorney)

The book also includes sample provisions you can add to your will or your revocable living trust. Getting the forms is just the first step. The next step is to discuss the forms and the sample provisions and any modifications you think might be necessary with your attorney. Note that many of the documents you need will probably not have to be created from scratch because your attorney undoubtedly will have his or her own standard forms. It will be less costly and less complicated for your attorney to make minor (in terms of drafting, not impact) modifications to his or her standard forms then draft an entirely new document. An added advantage to this is that your attorney's standard forms will already be tailored to accommodate your state's laws.

WHY HIRING AN ATTORNEY IS THE BEST WAY TO GO

This section heading may sound like a self-serving plug from an attorney, but it really is sound advice. Think about it. You most likely don't prescribe your own medication—you leave this to a competent professional who is qualified to administer to your physical needs. By the same token, you should not prescribe your own complex legal decisions unless you are an attorney specializing in estate planning.

An attorney will take care of all document preparation for you and supervise your signing of those documents. This is by far the best approach, but remember that you are entitled and encouraged to express your opinions and concerns and preferences about the issues that matter most to you. Also note that most lawyers have a comfort level with their own forms, templates, and language. That is fine so long as they tailor them to fully address your personal situation and the ramifications of your chronic illness.

If you cannot afford an attorney, follow the steps below to increase the likelihood that your documents will be effective. The word "likelihood" is used here deliberately. The tremendous variations in the laws of different states, the need for objective legal reasoning, the formalities of signing documents, and other complex matters are really difficult for you to address properly on your own, and a do-it-yourself approach can leave you vulnerable.

IF YOU CANNOT AFFORD AN ATTORNEY

Although this information was touched upon in Chapter 1, it bears repeating here because there is no substitute for getting qualified legal assistance to safeguard yourself, your assets, and your loved ones. If your financial situation does not allow you to hire an attorney, you can contact a local chapter of the organization that offers services to people with your chronic illnesses. Such organizations may be willing to sponsor local estate planning programs to help people whose resources are limited but whose need for legal advice is pressing. As discussed in Chapter 1, charitable organizations can also be encouraged to sponsor fairs and symposiums geared to explaining and reviewing the legal issues and concepts that are the subject of this book. Many of these organizations have experience recruiting attorneys, financial planners, accountants, and other advisers experienced in estate planning to participate in such events.

IF YOU CANNOT GET ANY PROFESSIONAL HELP

If your efforts to get professional assistance do not succeed, your last resort may be to tackle the matter yourself. Use the ideas in this book and obtain Word documents of forms and sample provisions from www.laweasy.com. Hopefully you have made notes to yourself while reading this book that you can use to help you fill out these forms. Type in all relevant information, changes, and corrections that are pertinent to you. If you don't have access to a computer, or have trouble typing, ask a friend to help you. When you have completed the forms, print and carefully review them. (It is easier to spot mistakes on a hard copy than on a computer screen.) The final draft of your documents should not have corrections penned in; make all revisions on the computer and print clean final documents reflecting all the changes you've made. Once that has been done, staple the form twice, once on the top left corner, and once on the top right corner. <u>NEVER</u> remove the staples from the document you print. It may invalidate it.

SIGNING DOCUMENTS IF YOUR VISION IS IMPAIRED

If you have vision problems, you should print the final documents in large type so that you can read them and demonstrate to the witnesses and notary that you can read them. If your vision impairment is so severe that someone must fill out the documents for you, it is likely that this person is also helping you read and review the information in this book and has already seen the discussion on handwriting issues in the previous chapter. This chapter includes an appendix with information that addresses how someone with vision impairment can sign valid documents and sample documents that can be attached to your estate planning documents.

HOW TO SIGN FINAL DOCUMENTS

Be aware that state laws differ significantly on this point and should be reviewed before any documents are signed and/or filed. As discussed in an earlier chapter, you can find this information in the reference section of your local library. Use the index to find the specific information you need, but ask the librarian to show you the updates, often called "pocket parts," that typically appear at the end of each volume. You can also try to find this information online.

Once your documents are prepared, there are several steps you must take to ensure that they are signed correctly and legally. Arrange to have two or three (depending on the forms) witnesses and a notary. None of the witnesses or the notary should be people named in the documents; also, they should not be related to you. Once you are all assembled in a clean quiet area, lay out each document. Then review and discuss the documents. Finally, sign them in front of each other (you should sign in the presence of the witnesses and notary and the witnesses should sign in front of you and each other). No one may leave the room during the signing process. Be sure to identify each document prior to signing it. Explain what the document accomplishes and why you are signing it. Before signing your will and revocable living trust (if you are using one), identify to the witnesses and notary all of the people you have named in these documents, describe your key assets, and explain in general terms how each document distributes these assets to the people you've named.

When you, the witnesses, and notaries are signing the documents, be sure to carefully read the notations under the signature lines and carefully follow the prompts listed in each form.

ONCE YOU'RE DONE, WHAT'S NEXT?

Once you have signed your documents, you must decide where they go:

❖ All original documents should be stored in a secure, fireproof location that is accessible to those who will serve as your agents and other fiduciaries.

❖ Prepare photocopies of the documents for each of your key advisers and fiduciaries. Don't unstaple the documents. Copy them by flipping each page one at a time so that the staples aren't disturbed.

❖ Sign only one copy of your will, and keep that original, preferably in a fireproof safe in your house.

❖ You can sign multiple originals of your living trust, but given the length of the document it's probably more practical to sign one original and distribute copies. If you've named a bank as trustee, the bank will want an original (but if you have enough assets that a bank or trust company will serve as trustee, you can also afford an attorney to do this).

❖ You may sign several original copies of your power of attorney, and if you truly trust your agent, you can give him or her a signed original. One copy should always be kept in a fireproof safe in your house, and one should be kept elsewhere (e.g., a safe deposit box).

❖ Sign several originals of the HIPAA release, health care proxy and living will. You should always give at least one original of each to your health care agent. If your first agent is someone living with you, it is a good idea to give a second original to someone named as a successor agent and lives elsewhere. You should also give your doctor or health care provider a photocopy to include with your medical records. One copy should always be kept at home in an easily and quickly accessible location in case of emergency.

ANNUAL REVIEW AND FOLLOW-UP

While some illnesses take a severe toll quite quickly, most chronic illnesses progress over time, affording you opportunities to revisit and refine your planning. Use these opportunities wisely. Annual reviews can ensure that new issues can be addressed, old decisions can be re-evaluated, and changes in circumstances and new legal developments can be incorporated. It is likely that your views and feelings about a range of issues (from personal care, to agents you have named, to other aspects of planning) will evolve as your illness lingers or progresses.

CHAPTER SUMMARY

This chapter addressed the final step in the estate planning process. Once you've thought through all your issues and made all your decisions, the final step is to complete and sign your documents. Great care should be taken in doing so. If there is any way in which you can obtain help from an attorney, ideally one specializing in estate planning, that will be the best for you. Whatever approach you use, great attention to detail and formalities is essential.

SAMPLE AFFIDAVITS FOR DOCUMENTS IF YOUR VISION IS IMPAIRED.

BLIND OR VISION-IMPAIRED CLIENT

Comment: *If the testator is vision impaired or blind, document the vision impairment and use an affidavit at the end of the will and other legal documents similar to the following. Take precautions to ensure that the testator understands the document being signed. Consider having the witnesses sign a separate affidavit confirming the precautions that were taken, which should include reading the entire document to the client to be sure he or she understands it. Applicable state law should be reviewed to determine what specific modifications, measures, or documents should be employed. Note that the form below uses the term "Testator," which might need to be changed to "Testatrix." The number of witnesses may have to be adjusted. If it is feasible to send an electronic version of the Will to the client in advance for them to have a computer program read it, this should be done. See the optional paragraph below. Alternatively, a very large print document could be sent, or the client may have a device to substantially enlarge the document to permit him or her to read it in advance. If any of these approaches are used, the provision concerning electronic reading should be modified to reflect this.*

Will Attestation Clause

Each of the undersigned Three (3) witnesses, individually and severally being duly sworn, depose and say: The within last will and testament ("Will"), consisting of [NUMBER OF PAGES] excluding this page, was read aloud to [TESTATOR NAME], the Testator, who is [LEGALLY BLIND OR DESCRIBE VISION-IMPAIRMENT]. Each page, after that page was so read, was initialed by the Testator, in the presence, sight and hearing of each of us. After all pages constituting the Will were read, Testator subscribed such Will by executing the Will in our presence, sight and hearing, the within named Testator, on [MONTH *DAY, *YEAR at *SIGN-ADDRESS].

Furthermore, Testator stated to the undersigned witnesses that Testator received in advance of the signing of this Will an electronic version of the Will which Testator was able to have electronically read to Testator so that Testator was familiar with the contents of the Will prior to the reading of this Will referred to above. [MODIFY AS REQUIRED]

Said Testator declared the instrument so subscribed to be such Testator's last will and testament. Each of the undersigned thereupon signed as a witness at the end of said last will and testament, at the request of said Testator. Such signings where in such Testator's presence and hearing, and were in the presence, sight and hearing, of each other of the witnesses.

Said Testator was, at the time of so executing said Will, over the age of Eighteen (18) years and, in the respective opinions of the undersigned, of sound mind, memory, and understanding and not under any restraint or in any respect incompetent to make a last will and testament, other than the vision impairment referred to above. The Testator could write and converse in the English language and was not suffering from any significant defect of mind, hearing, or speech, and did not appear to suffer from any other physical or mental impairment, which would affect Testator's capacity to make a valid will. Although the Testator has the vision issue noted above, since this Will was read out loud to the Testator, his defect of sight did not affect his capacity to understand the content of same or to make a valid will.

This Will was executed as a single original instrument and was not executed in counterparts.

Each of the undersigned was acquainted with said Testator at the time of the execution hereof, and makes this affidavit at such Testator's request. The within Will was shown to the undersigned Witnesses at the time this affidavit was made, and was examined by each of them as to the signature of said Testator and of the undersigned.

The foregoing instrument was executed by the Testator, and witnessed by each of the undersigned affiants under the supervision of [ATTORNEY NAME], Esq. an attorney-at-law.

POWER OF ATTORNEY ATTESTATION CLAUSE
FOR BLIND OR VISION-IMPAIRED GRANTOR

Comment: *Consider inserting this clause at the end of the power of attorney document and prior to the notary signature and seal. Research state law to determine if there is any specific requirement or guidance. For a standard pre-printed form, use insert "Power of Attorney Attestation Clause Attached" prior to the notary and witness lines. Many forms only are notarized and may not require a witness so modify the initial sentence below accordingly. Note that this form calls for each page of the power to be initialed by the vision impaired Grantor prior to execution. Standard forms do not require this step. If it is feasible to send an electronic version of the Power to the client in advance for them to have a computer program read it, this should be done. See the optional paragraph below. Alternatively, a very large print document could be sent, or the client may have a device to substantially enlarge the document to permit him or her to read it in advance. If any of these approaches are used, the provision concerning electronic reading should be modified to reflect this. If the Grantor has any significant physical or other impairment, read carefully and modify the language below. Note that this affidavit reflects a conclusion of the Grantor having contractual capacity which his higher then mere testamentary capacity. Some states may permit the validity of a power executed with the lower testamentary capacity standard. Unlike most powers this affidavit expressly contemplates that the power execution will be supervised by an attorney.*

Comment: SIGN ONLY ONE ORIGINAL BUT MAKE FIVE (5) CERTIFIED TRUE COPIES DATED THE SAME DATE AS THE ORIGINAL.

Each of the undersigned Two (2) witnesses, individually and severally being duly sworn, depose and say:

The power of attorney to which this Attestation Clause has been included and made part of the above power of attorney ("Power"), consisting of [*NUMBER OF PAGES], including this page, was read aloud to [GRANTOR NAME], Grantor, who is [LEGALLY BLIND; DESCRIBE VISION IMPAIRMENT].

Each page, after that page was so read, was initialed by the Grantor, in the presence, sight and hearing of each of the undersigned witnesses. After all pages constituting this Power were read, Grantor executed the Power by signing the signature page thereof, in our presence, sight and hearing, on [*MONTH, *DAY, *YEAR at *SIGN-ADDRESS].

Furthermore, Grantor stated to the undersigned witnesses that Grantor received in advance of the signing of this Power an electronic version of the Power which Grantor was able to have electronically read to Grantor so that Grantor was familiar with the contents of the Power prior to the reading of this Power referred to above. [MODIFY AS REQUIRED]

Said Grantor declared the instrument so executed to be such Grantor's durable power of attorney for financial matters. Each of the undersigned thereupon signed as a witness at the end of said Power at the request of said Grantor. Such signings where in such Grantor's presence and hearing, and were in the presence, sight and hearing, of each other of the witnesses.

Said Grantor was, at the time of so executing said Power, over the age of Eighteen (18) years and, in the respective opinions of the undersigned, of sound mind, memory, and understanding and not under any restraint or in any respect incompetent to execute a contractual agreement, other than the vision impairment referred to above. The Grantor could write and converse in the English language and was suffering from no significant defect of mind, hearing, or speech, and did not appear to suffer from any other physical or mental impairment, which would affect Grantor's contractual capacity [*CONFIRM CAPACITY*]. Although the Grantor has the vision issue noted above, since this Power was read out loud to the Grantor, Grantor's defect of sight did not affect his capacity to execute a valid durable power of attorney.

This Power was executed as a single original instrument and was not executed in counterparts. Only One (1) original Power was so executed but Five (5) copies thereof were made and certified to be true as of the date hereof, in accordance with Grantor's directions. Each of the undersigned was acquainted with said Grantor at such time, and makes this affidavit at such Grantor's request. The within Power was shown to the undersigned at the time this affidavit was made, and was examined by each of them as to the signature of said Grantor and of the undersigned.

The foregoing instrument was executed by the Grantor and witnessed by each of the undersigned affiants under the supervision of [*ATTORNEY NAME], Esq. an attorney-at-law.

LIVING WILL ATTESTATION CLAUSE
FOR BLIND OR VISION-IMPAIRED GRANTOR

Comment: *Consider inserting this clause at the end of both the living will and health proxy document, and prior to the notary signature and seal on each. Research state law to determine if there is any specific requirement or guidance. Note that this form calls for each page of the living will and health proxy to be initialed by the vision impaired Grantor prior to execution. If it is feasible to send an electronic version of the living will and health care proxy to the client in advance for him or her to have a computer program read it, this should be done. See the optional paragraph below. Alternatively, a very large print document could be sent, or the client may have a device to substantially enlarge the document to permit him or her to read it in advance (i.e., for a vision impaired client who is not blind). If any of these approaches are used, the provision concerning electronic reading should be modified to reflect this. If the Grantor has any significant physical or other impairment, read carefully and modify the language below. Note that this affidavit reflects a conclusion of the Grantor having contractual capacity which his higher then mere testamentary capacity. Some states may permit the validity of a living will and health proxy executed with the lower testamentary capacity standard, or perhaps even a special standard applicable to the authorization of health care decision making. Unlike most living wills, this affidavit expressly contemplates that the power execution will be supervised by an attorney. This affidavit is to supplement, to substitute for, the common affidavit signed by witnesses to a living will.*

Comment: SIGN ONLY ONE ORIGINAL BUT MAKE FIVE (5) CERTIFIED TRUE COPIES DATED THE SAME DATE AS THE ORIGINAL.

Each of the undersigned Two (2) witnesses, individually and severally being duly sworn, depose and say:

The [living will health care proxy] to which this Attestation Clause has been included and made part of the above living will ("Living Will"), consisting of [*NUMBER OF PAGES], including this page, was read aloud to [*GRANTOR-NAME], Grantor, who is [legally blind DESCRIBE VISION-IMPAIRMENT].

Each page, after that page was so read, was initialed by the Grantor, in the presence, sight and hearing of each of the undersigned witnesses. After all pages constituting this Living Will were read, Grantor executed the Living Will by signing the signature page thereof, in our presence, sight and hearing, on [*MONTH *DAY, *YEAR at *SIGN-ADDRESS].

Furthermore, Grantor stated to the undersigned witnesses that Grantor received in advance of the signing of this Living Will an electronic version of the Living Will which Grantor was able to have electronically read to Grantor so that Grantor was familiar with the contents of the Living Will prior to the reading of this Living Will referred to above. [MODIFY AS REQUIRED*]

Said Grantor declared the instrument so executed to be such Grantor's living will, statement of health care wishes. Each of the undersigned thereupon signed as a witness at the end of said Living Will at the request of said Grantor. Such signings where in such Grantor's presence and hearing, and were in the presence, sight and hearing, of each other of the witnesses.

Said Grantor was, at the time of so executing said Living Will, over the age of Eighteen (18) years and, in the respective opinions of the undersigned, of sound mind, memory, and understanding and not under any restraint or in any respect incompetent to execute a Living Will, other than the vision impairment referred to above. The Grantor could write and converse in the English language and was suffering from no significant defect of mind, hearing or speech, and did not appear to suffer from any other physical or mental impairment, which would affect Grantor's capacity to execute a living will [*CONFIRM NO IMPAIRMENT*]. Although the Grantor has the vision issue noted above, since this Living Will was read out loud to the Grantor, Grantor's defect of sight did not affect his capacity to make a valid living will.

This Living Will was executed as a single original instrument and was not executed in counterparts. Only One (1) original living will was so executed but Five (5) copies thereof were made and certified to be true as of the date hereof, in accordance with Grantor's directions.

Each of the undersigned was acquainted with said Grantor at such time, and makes this affidavit at such Grantor's request. The within Living Will was shown to the undersigned at the time this affidavit was made, and was examined by each of them as to the signature of said Grantor and of the undersigned.

The foregoing instrument was executed by the Grantor and witnessed by each of the undersigned affiants under the supervision of [*ATTORNEY NAME], Esq. an attorney-at-law.

HEALTH CARE PROXY ATTESTATION CLAUSE
FOR BLIND OR VISION-IMPAIRED GRANTOR

Comment: *Consider inserting this clause at the end of a health proxy document, and prior to the notary signature and seal. Research state law to determine if there is any specific requirement or guidance. Note that this form calls for each page of the health proxy to be initialed by the vision impaired Grantor prior to execution. If it is feasible to send an electronic version of the health care proxy to the client in advance for him or her to have a computer program read it, this should be done. See the optional paragraph below. Alternatively, a very large print document could be sent, or the client may have a device to substantially enlarge the document to permit him or her to read it in advance (i.e., for a vision impaired client who is not blind). If any of these approaches are used the provision concerning electronic reading should be modified to reflect this. If the Grantor has any significant physical or other impairment read carefully and modify the language below. Note that this affidavit reflects a conclusion of the Grantor having contractual capacity which his higher then mere testamentary capacity. Some states may permit the validity of a health proxy executed with the lower testamentary capacity standard, or perhaps even a special standard applicable to the authorization of health care decision making. Unlike most health proxies this affidavit expressly contemplates that the health care proxy execution will be supervised by an attorney. This affidavit is to supplement, to substitute for, the common affidavit signed by witnesses to a health care proxy.*

Comment: SIGN ONLY ONE ORIGINAL BUT MAKE FIVE (5) CERTIFIED TRUE COPIES DATED THE SAME DATE AS THE ORIGINAL.

Each of the undersigned Two (2) witnesses, individually and severally being duly sworn, depose and say:

The health care proxy to which this Attestation Clause has been included and made part of the above health care proxy ("Health Care Proxy"), consisting of [*NUMBER OF PAGES], including this page, was read aloud to [*GRANTOR NAME], Grantor, who is [LEGALLY BLIND* DESCRIBE VISION IMPAIRMENT].

Each page, after that page was so read, was initialed by the Grantor, in the presence, sight, and hearing of each of the undersigned witnesses. After all pages constituting this Health Care Proxy were read, Grantor executed the Health Care Proxy by signing the signature page thereof, in our presence, sight and hearing, on [*MONTH *DAY, *YEAR at *SIGN-ADDRESS].

Furthermore, Grantor stated to the undersigned witnesses that Grantor received in advance of the signing of this Health Care Proxy an electronic version of the Health Care Proxy which Grantor was able to have electronically read to Grantor so that Grantor was familiar with the contents of the Health Care Proxy prior to the reading of this Health Care Proxy referred to above. [MODIFY AS REQUIRED*]

Said Grantor declared the instrument so executed to be such Grantor's Health Care Proxy, appointment of a health care agent. Each of the undersigned thereupon signed as a witness at the end of said Health Care Proxy at the request of said Grantor. Such signings where in such Grantor's presence and hearing, and were in the presence, sight, and hearing, of each other of the witnesses.

Said Grantor was, at the time of so executing said Health Care Proxy, over the age of Eighteen (18) years and, in the respective opinions of the undersigned, of sound mind, memory, and understanding and not under any restraint or in any respect incompetent to execute a Health Care Proxy, other than the vision impairment referred to above. The Grantor could write and converse in the English language and was suffering from no significant defect of mind, hearing, or speech, and did not appear to suffer from any other physical or mental impairment, which would affect Grantor's capacity to execute a Health Care Proxy [*CONFIRM NO IMPAIRMENT*]. Although the Grantor has the vision issue noted above, since this Power was read out loud to the Grantor, Grantor's defect of sight did not affect his capacity to make a valid Health Care Proxy.

This Health Care Proxy was executed as a single original instrument and was not executed in counterparts. Only One (1) original Health Care Proxy was so executed but Five (5) copies thereof were made and certified to be true as of the date hereof, in accordance with Grantor's directions.

Each of the undersigned was acquainted with said Grantor at such time, and makes this affidavit at such Grantor's request. The within Health Care Proxy was shown to the undersigned at the time this affidavit was made, and was examined by each of them as to the signature of said Grantor and of the undersigned.

The foregoing instrument was executed by the Grantor and witnessed by each of the undersigned affiants under the supervision of [*ATTORNEY NAME], Esq. an attorney-at-law.

INDEX